PRAISE FOR

Orphans No More

I loved reading this book! True stories are often the best, and the message of this book is beyond most. Sandra conveys engaging adoption stories filled with truth, hope, and encouragement. Perfect for individual readers, small groups, and book clubs. *Orphans No More* is a beautiful, powerful resource.

—**KIM DE BLECOURT**, Author of *I Call You Mine: Embracing God's Gift of Adoption* and *Until We All Come Home: A Harrowing Journey, a Mother's Courage, a Race to Freedom*

Orphans No More is a beautifully crafted, honest account of one family's adoption journey. Through her vivid imagery and storytelling, Sandra Flach invites readers into God's story of adoption and redemption. Sandra captures the essence of the highs and lows that a family experiences when saying yes to adoption and does so with transparency and vulnerability. Sandra weaves her personal story together with the truth of God's Word and examines the ways we all are tempted to live as spiritual orphans. *Orphans No More* is a must-read for any family who has been touched by adoption or for anyone with a desire to love the orphaned and vulnerable. I closed the book refreshed, challenged, and in awe of the ways God moves heaven and earth to create family.

—**KAREN SPRINGS**, Author of *Adoption Through the Rearview Mirror: Learning from Stories of Heartache and Hope*, and Communications Lead at World Without Orphans

I have known Sandra Flach for a number of years, but I never knew her story. *Orphans No More* is a riveting story of a family with a call on their lives, a story of incredible perseverance, and a story of hearts full of love and compassion. With vulnerability and openness, Sandra allows us into the hard parts of creating a family by adoption. She also invites us to celebrate the successes. I highly recommend this book, not just for those touched by adoption, but for anyone with a heart and mind open to the crisis of orphaned children. It is written so well.

—JAYNE SCHOOLER,
Co-Author of *Wounded Children, Healing Homes*
and *Telling the Truth to Your Adopted or Foster Child*

Orphans No More is a must-read for anyone considering adoption or foster care. If you are a Christian and have suffered trauma, this is for you. If you work in ministry and want to truly understand the theology of adoption, read this book!

Sandra's story isn't just a retelling of her family's adoption. It's also a picture of the warfare of adoption. *Orphans No More* is a series of battles, victories, prayers, setbacks, and ultimately deliverance punctuating the fact that God sets the lonely in families. Each chapter has not only a well-told story, but a spiritual, emotional, and physical lesson as well.

Sandra weaves together the telling of the adoption of each of her children with her own struggles and triumphs in faith. Her vibrant and honest word pictures made me feel as if I were right there with her. Her journey impacted me on every page, building my faith and rehearsing victories from my own adoption journey.

The section of the book on the orphan spirit is eye-opening for any Christian. The teaching on the orphan spirit is the missing piece of the attachment parenting puzzle. Once you understand the orphan spirit in yourself and your child, the pieces of the puzzle fall into place.

The final section of the book—the testimonies from former orphans and foster children—is an amazing way to wrap things up. These stories will cause you to rejoice in the miracle-working power of God, our Father, whose end goal is for everyone to be orphans no more.

—KATHLEEN GUIRE, Former National Parent of the Year, Mother of Seven (four through adoption), ETC Parent Trainer, Author of *A Positive Adoption Story: The Door From Theology to Reality*

Sandra has written a book packed with so many layers of truth intertwined with the heart of God for the vulnerable of the earth and her humanity as weak and unable to carry out what God called her to do. She opens doors of revelation and understanding to the interactions of God and His love—fueled will for her children to be adopted with the realities of working through governmental systems and hurdles. She also reveals the love of God being poured out by His grace to her and through her and her family to love her children through their own brokenness. It is a remarkable account of one family's "boots on the ground" journey to manifest the heart of the Lord for the last, the least, and the lost.

—CHARLES AND MARY BETH ENGELHARDT, Abounding Love Christian Fellowship, Senior Pastors

Sandra is *such* a blessing to the foster care/adoption community, and *Orphans No More* is a treasure for the reader. In her book, Sandra shares her heart for adoption, foster care, and serving the Lord through her ministry. Sandra's writing is so engaging—the reader is twice transported to the Ukraine in the adoption of her four children. She shares the roller coaster of emotions and experiences that accompany international and kinship adoption. While sharing her journey, Sandra also shares the vulnerability of her lived experiences, beautifully weaving scripture and how her faith has carried her through her journey. As a bio mom, adoptive mom, and founder of an adoptive/foster care ministry/nonprofit organization, Sandra Flach has made a difference in the world. *Orphans No More* tells her story and shares her journeys of determination, hope, and faith.

—NATALIE VECCHIONE,
Adoptive Mom and Host of the *FASD Hope* Podcast

Those who choose adoption often find ourselves on the roller coaster of both sacrifice and redemption. Highs and lows are interspersed and reversed every single day. Thus, it is that joyful gain, painful loss, challenging transitions, and hope-filled new life thread throughout this inspiring story of Sandra Flach and her family of eight children, five of whom were enveloped into their lives through God's divine intervention. *Orphans No More* is a page-turning narrative of a couple who seek to follow God's path in establishing their family and faith. In the book's final chapters, we are reminded of our own tendencies to live as spiritual orphans and how being adopted into God's forever family changes us from the inside out. At its core, Flach's message is that we all have a deep need to belong. As believers growing in God's love and acceptance, we invite others to the table. I loved this book especially because three of my four children are also adopted, but I recommend it for anyone who longs for welcome as daughters and sons. Flach summarizes it well: "Walking in sonship requires more than just believing in God—we must know Him intimately." *Orphans No More* is a significant step towards that end.

—LUCINDA SECREST MCDOWELL,
Award-Winning Author of *Soul Strong* and *Life-Giving Choices*

This is an amazing story, not just about God's family, but also the how-to with respect to becoming an integral part of His family. God's family is an adoptive family. God is indeed the first adoptive Father and He sets the standard for us.

The story of Sandra and Wayne's journey through the adoption process (twice) are specific and detailed. Any family contemplating international adoption would be wise to read it. It's a journey that is not without bumps, potholes, twists, and turns. Like most worthwhile things in life, family requires hard work, determination, and an unshakeable faith in our Lord. Sandra describes in stunning detail the trials and challenges as well as the path to success.

One nugget from the book revolves around understanding the impact of trauma on the life of a child coming from a hard place. The author talks about how her only regret was not knowing how to parent a child with a trauma history. Simply knowing that you need to parent differently is not enough. One needs to know *how* to parent differently. Understanding the characteristics of a trauma competent parent and working hard to implement those strategies will go a long way to ensuring a successful transition. Chapter 21 outlines a number of different resources.

The narratives continually refer to Scripture as a foundation for this "trip." Insights, valuable for life, abound. One was, "We had forgotten the miracles of the past because we focused only on our present circumstances." Another says, "The fruit yielded through obedience will forever be my treasure."

The author challenges the reader, especially the believer, with questions like: "What are we living for? Are we investing our God-given gifts back into His Kingdom? Are we living for ourselves or for Jesus?"

I believe the most impactful part of the book lies in chapters 22-25. These relate to a condition we were all born into, a condition I refer to as orphanism. The orphan spirit runs amuck in this world. Sandra does a great job in describing many of the characteristics we see that describe an orphan spirit but she doesn't leave it there. She outlines the scriptural foundation for adoption and from that we can see the parallel process for our own lives as to whether or not we have been called to adopt. When we come to the realization, like the one with Slava, we are all wired for survival. That indeed, "As Christians, we are called to love and lay down our lives for others—this is adoption."

In the final part of the book, we read about the miraculous transformation from orphan to son. This transformation is not simply about a parent adopting a child, but the critical piece is about the metamorphosis as a Christian. Our adoption into the family of God releases our identity as children of God and all the responsibilities and benefits that ensue.

This book is a placeholder for every parent wanting to adopt. The bigger picture is this book exposes orphanism for what it really is and outlines a pathway for all of us to be *Orphans No More*.

—RUBY M. JOHNSTON,
LAMb International/Global Capacity Building Network, Co-Founder
ILDC Ukraine and ILDC Kyrgystan, Co-Founder
WWO Executive Team, Capacity Building Coordinator

Orphans
No More

*you are a
chosen + dearly loved
child of God !
Sandra Flack
Eph. 1:3-5*

BROOKSTONE
PUBLISHING GROUP

Orphans No More
A Journey Back to the Father
Sandra Flach

Copyright © 2021

Brookstone Publishing Group
P.O. Box 211, Evington, VA 24550
BrookstoneCreativeGroup.com

ISBN: 978-1-949856-38-5 (paperback)
978-1-949856-39-2 (epub)

Ordering Information:
Special discounts are available on quantity purchases by corporations,
associations, and others. For details, contact
Brookstone Publishing Group at the address above.

Orphans
No More

A JOURNEY BACK
TO THE FATHER

SANDRA FLACH

BROOKSTONE
PUBLISHING GROUP

To my Heavenly Father,
to my husband, Wayne,
to my children and grandchildren.

CONTENTS

ACKNOWLEDGMENTS

To my wonderful, amazing husband, Wayne, who was the first to demonstrate the unconditional love of God to me. Your love, forgiveness, kindness, and adoration have brought such healing to my heart. You are my best friend. Thank you for your support and encouragement for more than thirty-three years of marriage as we raised eight children, homeschooled, launched a ministry, and finally got this book written!

To my eight amazing children whom God has blessed me with: Wayne Jr., Curtis, Missy, Sierra, Andrii, Anna, Jordan, and Slava. I have learned so much from each of you and look forward to witnessing the plans God has for you.

To Missy, our first adopted daughter, thank you for extending grace and forgiveness to us. We had no idea how to parent a kid with trauma back in 1999. You have blossomed into an amazing young woman in spite of our parenting failures. Thank you for allowing us the opportunity to re-do our relationship with the focus on connection.

To Andrii, the first born of our Ukrainian crew. You have been my hero since the very first day I met you at the orphanage in Ukraine. Your bravery, determination, and selflessness are an inspiration to me and all who know you. Thank you for saying no to the Chicago family and yes to us. Being your mom is one of the greatest privileges of my life.

To my daughter, Sierra, thank you for your editing efforts and encouragement. When you told me the book was good and that I should be proud, your words meant the world to me.

To my daughters-in-love, Kerri and Lauren. Then thank you for loving my sons and blessing me with five precious grandchildren. Iona, Aidan, Owen, Joseph, and Reya are my greatest treasures.

To my pastors, Chuck and Marybeth Engelhardt, thank you for your encouragement, support, and covering in all God has called me to do, including writing this book. Pastor Chuck, thank you for your edits and advice, especially in the areas of Scripture.

To the ladies in my life whom I'm blessed to call friends: Lauri, Kathi, Deb, Crystal, and all my Bible study gals. Your encouragement, support, prayers, and friendship make the journey of life richer, more enjoyable and endurable.

To my fellow authors, Kim de Blecourt and Kathleen Guire, thank you for your encouragement, advice, expertise, and friendship. You gave me the courage to move forward and finish this project.

To my patient writing coach, Larry J. Leech II, thank you for teaching me about the writing process. I learned so much from you over the nine-month process of rewriting my manuscript. I'm grateful for your tutelage.

To the inspirational individuals who provided testimonies found inside the pages of this book: Mandy Litzke, Daniel Kaggwa, Anu Silas, Jacob Sturges, Diana Pryhodko, and George Ebenezer. It is an honor to know you and a privilege to share your stories. You each truly are sons and daughters of God.

To my Heavenly Father, thank you for not leaving me an orphan but adopting me into your family through the cross of Christ and making me a joint-heir with Jesus. For filling me with your Holy Spirit and transforming me into a daughter of the King— your chosen, wanted, and dearly loved daughter! Thank you for pouring out blessings in my life, which include my most treasured possessions: my husband, children, and grandchildren. Thank you for creating me with a purpose, for writing down all the days of my life in your book, which included me writing this book. I wrote because you said to, and I pray you will be glorified in and through it. Use it for your glory.

The events in the following pages are shared with permission from the family members and friends mentioned by name. Because of the sensitivity of some information, and my desire to protect the identities of certain individuals, the names of several people and places have been changed.

Foreword

When we walk in obedience, the Father pours out his blessings on our lives. Sandra Flach has been given an abundance of blessings in family, ministry, and media. But this comes as no surprise to those who know her.

Obedience is the heartbeat of Sandra Flach's life. Through her riveting storytelling in *Orphans No More*, we hear many familiar themes about adoption . . . complicated birth families, confusing paperwork, courtroom intrigue, spiritual opposition, waiting and wondering, and personal sacrifice. But most of all, what we see over the life of the author is an absolute commitment to obedience. Sandra and her husband had the idyllic life of a "nice Christian family," but they knew that the call to a walk with Christ meant so much more. It meant absolute surrender to his command to care for the fatherless child.

Rather than keep the comfortable life they led with their biological children, the Flachs answered in obedience when a child in the extended family needed adoption. Before long, God had called them overseas to a years-long process of receiving four more children. And in the case of the Flachs, their commitment and obedience would grow deeper and deeper as their last adoption brought even more significant "special needs" into the family.

As a friend and co-laborer with Sandra for over a decade, I have the vantage point of seeing her children in the "after" and I see only the beauty. From where I sit, a challenging child is a delightful messenger of God's perfect creativity. Another, I've watched grow into an amazing man of God and family leader. To me, it all seems lovely. But Sandra takes us inside the real story of how each of the steps in this family's journey required an obedience far greater than the step before. And one bedrock truth drove that obedience . . . the Word of God.

Woven in the pages of every chapter of this wonderful book is Scripture. *Orphans No More* is really about the Word of God and one woman's resolute commitment to it. Sandra clung steadfastly to Scripture and used it to pave her every step of her journey. She compellingly lays out for us terror and destruction of the "orphan spirit." And she leads us to great victory with the Gospel of Adoption and its meaning for every child, including herself. Sandra transparently reveals her own painful past and how she overcame the same fear and rejection felt by orphans. Sandra has let the Word of God heal her *and* her children, and her incredible spirit-filled reflections can do the same for you. Read on with joy and anticipation.

—JODI JACKSON TUCKER,
Author of *Second Mother: A Bible Study Experience for Foster and Adoptive Mothers* and *Fasten Your Sweet Belt: 10 Things You Need to Know About Older Child Adoption.*

Introduction

"Even before he made the world, God loved us and chose us in Christ to be holy and without fault in his eyes. God decided in advance to adopt us into his own family by bringing us to himself through Jesus Christ."

EPHESIANS 1:3-5 NLT

The cross of Christ is *our* adoption process. Adoption is not a man-made plan B but God's plan A from the beginning, even before He made the world. His unchanging plan has always been to *adopt us* into His family. He would not leave us as orphans. Through Jesus Christ, He would adopt us and make us His children. We would be orphans no more.

The physical adoption of a child into a family is a model of our spiritual adoption. I've been a Christian for more than thirty years, but it wasn't until my husband and I adopted our children that I began to understand my salvation, my identity, and my destiny. Every adoption is a God-story, so in the following pages I will intertwine God's Word with stories from our family's three adoption journeys. In the second half I will illustrate the parallels between physical and spiritual adoption, the orphan spirit, and the spirit of adoption to sonship.

Wayne and I have been called heroes by people who believe we've done a wonderful thing—adopting children. I'm not fooled by this well-meaning praise because I know this story is not about anything great we have done but about what God has done. Fellow adoptive mom Eileen Mestas has said many times, "It's His story for His glory." And that's why I'm sharing our story. Over the past decade, I have met countless foster and adoptive families and orphan ministry leaders from around the world. I've had the privilege of interviewing many of them on my *Orphans No More* radio show and podcast. Every one of their stories is a God story. God called them. They stepped out in obedience, and God equipped them. Orphans are now sons and daughters. God gets the glory. So, here is my family's story.

CHAPTER 1

Andrii's Story

"God sets the lonely in families . . ."

PSALM 68:6 NIV

Remain an orphan or become a son. Andrii stood at a crossroads. Our son chose to stay orphaned. He was nine; his sister, Anna, seven. Because of his decision she would endure as an orphan too. The reason remained a mystery for four years until Andrii stood in church in 2011 to give a testimony. I had no clue what my fourteen-year-old son would say, but his opening line captivated me. "I now know the love of God."

Andrii shared about living in a Ukrainian orphanage. Then he explained how he and Anna traveled to Chicago twice on an orphan hosting program. I was riveted—my son was about to reveal the secret.

Andrii described the American host family as "nice." They even wanted to adopt him and Anna, but not their three-year-old sibling, Sergey. The younger boy remained back in Ukraine, too young for hosting and he also had medical needs requiring multiple surgeries. The Chicago family hadn't met him and were only interested in adopting Andrii and his sister.

Though Andrii knew about Sergey, he'd never met him. His younger brother lived in a baby house several miles away from the orphanage for school age children. At age nine, Andrii said no to

3

the host family because he wanted his biological siblings together, although they'd never been all together.

Andrii shared that three months after returning to the orphanage from Chicago the Flachs came to Ukraine. When the orphanage director explained to him this American couple wanted to adopt all three siblings, he agreed to the adoption. Andrii concluded his testimony by reading John 3:16 and restated how he now knew the love of God.

I was a puddle of mush. He returned to his seat and I wrapped my arms around my son and squeezed him tight. Mystery solved. A proud mama-moment for sure.

To this day I am in awe of the selfless decision made by a nine-year-old boy. I believe the Lord honored Andrii's sacrifice by providing his heart's desire—a family for his family.

Four years earlier, Wayne and I were flying down a Ukrainian highway in a tiny European auto. Seated up front, our adoption facilitator and translator, Alexandra—a blonde, petite powerhouse. Her tall, lean brother, Stanislav, drove. The thirty-something duo would become family to us in the weeks ahead. Inspector Svetlana, a Ukrainian government official, squeezed in the backseat with us—her presence required for the first meeting with the children we had chosen to adopt.

Stanislav turned the car onto an old, bumpy, village road two hours outside Kyiv. Svetlana, anxious to practice her English, filled the air with animated conversation. In her thick, Ukrainian accent, she offered some background information on the kids. Inspector Svetlana revealed nine-year-old Andrii and seven-year-old Anna traveled to Chicago twice on a hosting program.

My thoughts, busy jumping around like the car avoiding potholes, became focused on the inspector's report. I knew about hosting programs where orphans spend several weeks in the U.S. on holiday with a host family. The children are told it's a vacation and a chance to experience a new culture. But the real goal is for a connection to be made between the children and the host family, which could lead to adoption. I asked Svetlana why the host family didn't pursue adopting these children after hosting them for two summers. She said the family wanted to adopt the children, but the older boy didn't agree to the adoption.

Because of his age, Andrii had a say in whether or not he wanted to be adopted. Questions swirled in my head. Why wouldn't Andrii say yes to the opportunity to be adopted by the Chicago family? I'm sure they provided exciting opportunities and experiences for him and Anna while they were in the states. Was something wrong with these kids? My most startling thought: *Why would he say yes to us on our first meeting when he had said no to the other American family?*

In two years of planning for this day, I never considered a child we wanted to adopt wouldn't want to be adopted. Now, we were traveling through Ukrainian farmland and navigating around horse-drawn carts loaded down with sacks of vegetables and sunflower seeds to a meeting that was key to the rest of the adoption process. On this day, Wayne and I would have to say yes to these kids and they would have to say yes to us.

Together our yesses would start the marathon of paperwork and appointments necessary before we could cross the finish line as a forever family. The clock was ticking in my head while I calculated the four short weeks until the Ukrainian government would shut down for the holidays. I decided we needed to turn that little cramped sardine can around and head back to Kyiv so we could pick different kids. Kids who would say yes. The sardine can, however, kept speeding south toward the orphanage in a village I'll call Kasylviv.

When we arrived, the swirls in my head shifted to what was in front of me. Entering the World War II-era cement building the odor of fermented cabbage permeated the air. I had to stifle the desire to pull my turtleneck sweater over my nose. Inside we were welcomed by hospitable orphanage staff and escorted to an office where we sat on hard wooden chairs and waited for whatever would happen next.

Like a timid but curious kitten, little Anna came into the room first and sat next to us. Wayne looked at her, at me, and in awe declared, "She's beautiful." I smiled and handed her a mini Magna-doodle toy from my coat pocket. She swiped it and drew a little house on it. Her main caregiver, a well-dressed middle-aged woman, entered the office in tears. Alexandra translated her emotional words, "Anna is a lovely girl." I swallowed hard. For the first time I realized our gain would be someone's loss. The children may be orphaned, but there are people who cared about them.

Minutes later, Anna took my hand and whisked me off for a tour. With pride she showed me her little bed with a huge stuffed dog flopped over it. I knew visitors were not permitted in this part of the orphanage and was surprised the staff allowed her to show me around. After we returned to the office, Andrii strutted in and shook our hands. Through the translator we were officially introduced. Twice he asked her to repeat Wayne's name. This kid was paying attention to details while he evaluated us. Andrii showed us a small photo album from his trip to Chicago and we shared pictures of our home and family.

The fairytale experience was interrupted when Alexandra peered at us and said, "Do you want to adopt these children?"

Okay, no more playing around, back to serious business. The arduous adoption process included the prospective parents filing paperwork with the State Department for Adoption (SDA) in Kyiv requesting to adopt the child/children they had chosen. The official request was the first of many hoops we would have to jump through.

Because of the impending holiday shutdown, Alexandra wanted to submit the paperwork that day. Smiling, Wayne and I looked at each other and together declared, "Yes!" Our answer triggered a flurry of events. Back into the sardine can we went speeding off to a town I'll call Bryankiv for our official visit with three-year-old Sergey.

We arrived at the baby house midday. Wayne and I were escorted to an upstairs room to meet our boy. The area, furnished with gym mats and riding toys, an unexpected surprise in an orphanage. A colorful plastic ball pit, the kind in fast food restaurants back home, occupied the center. We stared at the equipment—shocked by what we saw.

My attention turned when the door opened. A woman in a white lab coat led a tiny boy into the room. Little Sergey hid behind the doctor. She pointed to the toys. Avoiding us, he hopped on a red plastic car and scooted around the room.

Alexandra, anxious to file our paperwork at the SDA, rushed us through the visit. But it didn't matter—Sergey captured our hearts with his crossed eyes and crooked back. We said yes to him too.

Andrii must have said yes to us also because the adoption moved forward, setting off an intense six-week process, which concluded with the adoption of all three children. I didn't have time to think about Andrii's decision. Once home, the demands of our family of nine consumed my time and pushed the mystery to the back of my mind. There it remained until the day he gave his testimony.

CHAPTER 2

Chosen

"God loved us and chose us in Christ . . ."

EPHESIANS 1:4 NLT

Wayne and I believed God called us to adopt a sibling group from Ukraine. Siblings are harder to place because not all adoptive families feel they can handle the responsibility of more than one child. The thought of splitting up families because no one wanted them as a group broke our hearts.

God created the family unit for children to germinate, grow, and blossom within. It's the place where life-long relationships are cultivated, lessons are learned, and love abounds. Roots go deep in a family. Or at least that's how our Creator intended for it to work.

When I was in grade-school my parents divorced. My brother and I lived with our mom. Aunts, uncles, cousins, and grandparents lived nearby and were all part of our daily lives. Wayne grew up in a family with four siblings. His grandfather was a pastor. The family spent lots of time together in church. To this day we live within a thirty-mile radius of our siblings.

With family foundational in our lives, Wayne and I believed keeping siblings together was paramount. We also figured as long as we were adopting, we might as well jump in all the way. Our dossier and Immigration and Naturalization Service (INS) application requested approval to adopt a sibling set of two. After eight months of tedious paperwork, which included background checks, medical exams for Wayne and I and all four of our kids living at home, and a home study, our dossier was finally sent to Ukraine in July 2005. Our adoption application was approved by the SDA two months later.

The next step in the process: wait to receive a letter from Ukraine inviting us to travel for an appointment with the SDA. At this meeting, prospective adoptive parents view pictures of orphans to choose from. The idea of catalog shopping for kids seemed surreal, but everything within me ached for this appointment. I longed to see the faces of the children God chose for our family.

Hoping to travel to Ukraine any minute, we anxiously waited for notification. Every day for weeks I pounced on the mail and ran down every UPS, DHL, and FedEx truck in my neighborhood. After a ten-week eternity a letter arrived from Ukraine in November notifying us that all appointments for international adoption were filled for the calendar year. We were placed on a waiting list for 2006. Not what I wanted the letter to say. In an effort to give my mind a break from all the adoption anticipation, I threw myself into the holiday season. Convincing myself Ukraine will be beautiful in the winter, I expected an invitation to travel at the beginning of the new year.

In January we were notified that Ukraine temporarily closed their adoption program for reorganization. Frustrated and disappointed we waited again. I added *wait* to the list of four-letter words I detested. Feeling our future was on hold, but having no other choice, we got on with our daily lives. This was easier for Wayne to do because he went to work every day managing the family construction business. I remained home teaching our four children: Wayne Jr. 16, Melissa 15, Curtis 13, and Sierra 9. With each passing day I noticed empty seats around our homeschool table. A glaring reminder, children were missing from our family.

Faith sustained me through the agonizing wait. But every passing month felt tortuous. May 2006 arrived and with it came discouragement as well as the expiration of all documents in our dossier. One year into the adoption process and I had to redo our entire file and pay all the processing fees again. Background checks, medical exams, home study—every piece of paper had to be updated. With trepidation I approached the dossier update, but renewed determination and fervent prayer fueled my mission. I begged the Lord to move the mountain blocking us from our children.

As I scaled the paperwork mountain again, I sensed we should increase the number of children we applied for. I approached my husband about adopting four children instead of two. Wayne got that deer-in-the-headlights look. Four children at once? The idea was a bit too far beyond his comfort zone. After some discussion and prayer, we compromised. I sent in our updated dossier with a request to adopt three children. The waiting continued, but now I enjoyed a sense of peace. Not only were we a step closer to our kids, we were more in line with God's plan.

The months dragged. I soaked up Scripture, prayed desperate prayers, fasted, blew a shofar, and cried on my best friend's shoulder. With audacity I reminded the Lord—and myself—He was the one who called us to adopt. We put our yes on the table and now waited for Him to accomplish His purposes (Isaiah 44:8). He sets the lonely in families (Psalm 68:6). We were a family waiting for the lonely. He calls believers to care for orphans (James 1:27). How can we care for them if we can't even get to them?

After pointing God to His own Word, I begged Him to open the door to our kids. Praying the Word has been powerful for me. The last day of October the door finally opened. We learned our appointment at the SDA in Kyiv was scheduled for November 29, 2006.

In all those excruciating months of waiting, God was at work preparing my heart for the children who He had chosen to place in our family. While I devoured my Bible and journaled, I also read books about adoption, attachment, and Fetal Alcohol Spectrum Disorder—a range of birth defects caused by maternal alcohol consumption common in children adopted from Eastern Europe.

Above all, I prayed for the children. I asked the Lord to prepare their hearts for us and to prepare our hearts for them. In less than four weeks, Wayne and I would walk into the SDA in Kyiv, look at pitiful pictures of orphans, and pick out our children. The task seemed overwhelming. God knew who our kids were, but how would *we* know? What if we messed up and picked the wrong ones? Our only option—trust the Lord would guide us.

The days of November inched by. In an attempt to push them along faster, I filled the time with a frenzy of planning, shopping, and packing. No small feat considering we would be traveling overseas with all four of our children: Wayne Jr. now 17, Missy 16, Curtis 14, and Sierra who celebrated her tenth birthday a week earlier. Wayne and I were not planning to bring them on the trip at first. But during the lengthy wait, God inspired us to take them along. Now they were excited about the escapade ahead.

A crowd of suitcases occupied our living room stuffed with winter garb, books, and other essentials. With the wheels of the adoption process finally greased, I wasn't about to leave anything to chance. Our flight was scheduled for the Sunday after Thanksgiving. We would go to church, get prayed over, leave service early, pack into the church van, and drive the two hours from upstate to John F. Kennedy International Airport in New York City. This timetable got us there four hours before boarding time.

Much to Wayne's dismay, I booked a direct flight from JFK to Boryspil International Airport in Kyiv. He preferred layovers because they provided an opportunity to walk and stretch. But I wouldn't permit layovers or flight delays to stand in my way. On the plane, I relaxed for the first time in eighteen months. The next stop, Kyiv, Ukraine.

Our family emerged from the Boryspil airport weary from ten hours on a plane but wired for the adventure. Alexandra, adoption facilitator extraordinaire, welcomed us with hugs. She led us to the parking lot and stuffed us, brood and baggage, onto a minibus.

Wayne and I and our four kids spent the first forty-eight hours in Kyiv settling into our home away from home—a modern apartment. Typical rentals are tiny, dingy, and reminiscent of the 1940s. I felt content with the comfortable accommodations: two spacious bedrooms, a living room with pull-out couch, large kitchen with up-to-date appliances, and a modern bathroom. The second story looked down on Khreshchatyk Street, Kyiv's main boulevard.

Kyiv was fascinating—rich in history and the landscape adorned with centuries old ornate churches. We experienced a bit of cultural confusion on our sight-seeing excursions. Spellbound by the ancient architecture one moment and shocked by a barrage of electronic billboards the next. Flashing flat-screen ads didn't quite fit with the babushkas seated on wooden crates selling sunflower seeds to survive. Though I reveled in the sights and smells of Kyiv, the only thing I could think about was our appointment at the SDA.

Appointment day arrived. November 29, 2006. I dreamed of this moment for almost two years. Wayne and I woke up feeling anxious. Jet lag, the need for coffee, and the 9:00 a.m. appointment had us on edge. In hushed tones we prayed together not wanting to wake our sleeping kids. Wayne asked God for our new children to be near Kyiv. Since we didn't yet know whom we would adopt, we also didn't know where they lived. The kids could be anywhere in Ukraine. My doubtful mind dismissed Wayne's practical prayer.

During all those months of waiting, I spent countless hours researching Ukrainian adoption. Most families fly or take an overnight train to Odessa or Donetsk or some other far away area. I didn't care where our kids were—I would travel anywhere to get them.

After we prayed, Wayne nor I said much. Lost in our own thoughts and silent prayers, we headed down to meet Alexandra on the street. Our lives were about to change forever.

Alex motioned to a white European auto idling nearby. We slid into the backseat. She hopped into the front and introduced us to her brother, Stanislav. He knew five English words—*yes*, *no*, and *I don't know*—but drove with competence.

The traffic congestion made the two-minute drive to the SDA take forever. We parked in the shadow of St. Michael's golden-domed monastery. Alexandra coached us for the appointment. The instruction of utmost importance: Inquire which region the chosen children were in. She explained with a sense of urgency the need to make the necessary travel arrangements for us to meet our new kids. My mind focused on the paramount task before us. Getting out of the car, the chilly November air awakened my senses. We stepped across the cobblestone street and entered the building.

The hall leading to the meeting room was dotted with other prospective parents and their facilitators. Everyone spoke in whispers and listened for our numbers to be called. Like cats poised to pounce, Wayne and I were ready. Alex signaled to us. Our turn. Because of the revised adoption process, facilitators were not permitted to attend the appointment with their families, so Alexandra waited for us in the hallway.

Inside the meeting room we were greeted by two young Ukrainian women. One a translator and the other a psychologist. They invited us to sit at a small, wooden table across from them. Wayne reached for my hand. We took our places and waited for instructions.

The psychologist held a batch of folders—each representing a child waiting for a family. I searched their faces for any kind of emotion but found none. I swallowed and tried to smile. The psychologist placed a pile of ten folders on the table. Through the translator she asked, "What age and gender do you want to adopt?" This question baffled me. This information was spelled out in our dossier, which lay in front of them.

Sensing we should play along, Wayne indicated we wanted a boy and a girl. I quickly added we were approved to adopt three children. My response triggered some excitement from the two stoic women. The psychologist grabbed a file from the desk behind her and placed three little "mug shots" before of us. She rattled off, "Andrii, boy age nine; Anna, girl age seven; and Sergey, boy age three."

A boy age three? When I daydreamed about our children in Ukraine the littlest was always a girl. The idea of a tiny boy felt disorienting. Wrestling with the desire for a girl but the possibility of a boy, I asked to see more pictures. We kept the three siblings' photos in front of us. The psychologist placed more photographs on the table: two girls, ages eleven and twelve; a boy and a girl; two boys.

I stopped listening as the trail seemed to grow cold. I kept looking at those three sad faces in the first pictures. In that moment, while praying a silent prayer for help, I'm certain I heard the Lord answer. Maybe I heard it in my heart instead of with my ears, but I heard it, *These three are the least of these.*

Wayne nudged me and whispered, "What do you think?"

Letting go of my desire for the youngest to be a girl, I took a deep breath. Knowing he might be less than thrilled with my choice of three kids when there were several options for just two, I said, "I think it's these three."

Without hesitation Wayne agreed wholeheartedly. "I think you're right."

His response surprised me, and I sat there in awe of what God had just done.

When we told the translator and psychologist we wanted to adopt the three siblings, the two women smiled for the first time. Both jumped from their seats and scrambled for the necessary documents. Beaming, the translator said, "You must care about the children to choose three."

I smiled back surprised by their enthusiasm. As instructed by Alex, we inquired about the region the kids were in. The psychologist opened their file and read, "Kyiv region."

Wayne nudged me. He would have high-fived Jesus if possible. I couldn't speak. God confirmed these are the children who He chose for our family.

The translator printed the region and district on a piece of paper and gave it to us. We smiled and uttered our best *spah-see-bah* or thank you in Russian.

Wayne and I emerged feeling triumphant. We knew our kids' names and had seen their faces. With pride, I handed Alexandra the paper. Her countenance changed from pleasure to concern when she read the information. Something didn't seem right. I searched Alex's face trying to decipher the problem.

My heart and my stomach felt like they just bottomed out on a roller coaster. Noticing our confusion Alex attempted to reassure us, "It will be okay."

I was not convinced.

CHAPTER 3

The Battle to Bring our Kids Home

"For when your faith is tested, your endurance has a chance to grow. So let it grow, For when your endurance is fully developed, you will be strong in character And ready for anything."

JAMES 1:3-4 NLT

The international adoption process varies by country. In Ukraine, the procedure seems to change moment by moment. Prior to the 2006 program restructure, families could choose the region and even the orphanage to adopt from. Some regions were notorious for disapproving of foreigners adopting *their* children. Government officials in those areas were difficult to work with. Adoption facilitators and families avoided those places.

By the time we traveled in November 2006, the process had been revised. First, a family chose a child at the SDA appointment. Then, the family was told the location of the child. This new process eliminated the option for families to avoid problematic regions.

Minutes after our appointment at the SDA, we huddled in the hallway with Alexandra. She explained her concern. "The children are in Kyiv Region. But the older two are in Kasylviv."

Alexandra described Kasylviv as one of those notorious areas facilitators and families avoided. Government officials in that district disapprove of international adoption. Everything around me faded. The clusters of families and facilitators dotting the corridor around us disappeared. My entire being zeroed in on the mission before us—bringing home our kids.

Although I had only glanced at their pictures and heard their names, my mama-bear claws came out. Nothing would keep me from my children. However, my countenance must have betrayed my bravado. With sympathetic eyes Alexandra again offered an unconvincing, "It will be okay."

Stanislav dropped Wayne and I back at the apartment. The pair sped off so Alex could make arrangements for us to meet the children. We watched their little car disappear down the street. I shivered—but not from the cold. Somewhere out there a battle was brewing in a place called Kasylviv.

All adoptions in Ukraine begin and end in the city of Kyiv, but most of the process occurs in the district where the orphanage was located and near the child's place of birth. Documents such as birth certificates, court decrees, and passport applications need signatures from various local government officials.

We were thankful the youngest child, three-year-old Sergey, lived in a baby orphanage in the village of Bryankiv. This institution, not far from Kyiv, processed adoptions often. Alex and her team had facilitated adoptions from Sergey's orphanage before. We didn't anticipate any problems there. Andrii and Anna, however, were in the dreaded district of Kasylviv.

Alexandra learned the two older children would be the first adopted out of the orphanage in Kasylviv. This didn't seem possible to me. In 2005, approximately 98,000 orphans lived in Ukraine. About 5,200 of them were adopted the same year.[1] The orphanage

1 Ministry of Family, Youth and Sport of Ukraine, National Report, Kyiv 2007.

sat two hours outside the capital city. I found it hard to believe not one of these official adoptions happened in Kasylviv. However, when Inspector Svetlana asked Alexandra to process her portion of the paperwork, I started to believe it.

An inspector holds the responsibility of preparing adoption documents in a district. Svetlana, however, didn't know how to fill out the forms. She preferred popping my Hershey Kisses into her mouth while watching Alex complete the paperwork. Svetlana chatted away about her husband being a professor at the University of Connecticut, her kids attending college in the states, and how much she loved American chocolate.

Our documents were prepared in record time thanks to Alexandra. Svetlana only signed her name. An unusual situation, but it worked to our benefit. We didn't have to wait for the bogged down bureaucracy of a former Soviet Socialist Republic. At least not yet. We were grateful for Inspector Svetlana. We had a friend in Kasylviv after all.

Alex's initial concern about the region seemed unfounded. We visited Andrii and Anna a few times each week. Inspector Svetlana, the orphanage director, staff, and even the hospitable woman in the orphanage office all welcomed us. We were offered food, invited to stay for special events, allowed to play with the other children, and permitted to visit as long as we wanted.

During the long months of waiting to travel, I researched the Ukrainian adoption process. I knew we weren't permitted in certain parts of the orphanage. I knew we were not supposed to interact with the other orphans. The staff at the baby house in Bryankiv understood the rules. The workers in Kasylviv didn't, which worked in our favor—at first.

Wayne and I traveled to Kasylviv almost a dozen times. We spent the two-hour car ride snuggled in the backseat. Stanislav drove while Alex explained adoption details and Ukrainian news. Each time, they dropped us at the orphanage and sped off.

While Wayne and I spent time with Andrii and Anna, Alexandra processed adoption paperwork in town. We didn't know what to expect during these visits with our kids. Sometimes we were alone with them drawing and playing hide-and-seek. Other times more orphan kids joined us. They were curious about the funny talking Americans.

All the children loved our digital camera. Andrii, Anna, and their friends begged to have their picture taken. They looked at themselves in the tiny camera screen, laughed, and posed again. The children never tired of this game.

If weather permitted, we played in the yard on archaic play-ground equipment. Inside the orphanage we experienced the warmth of family. Outside we sensed a harsh coldness. It wasn't from the weather.

On a cold December morning, Wayne and I and our four kids headed to Kasylviv. After two weeks in Ukraine, Wayne Jr., Missy, Curtis, and Sierra were about to meet their new siblings. Most days our crew stayed behind in the apartment and slept the day away. Not much room in the backseat for six people anyway.

On this day, however, Alexandra and Stanislav picked us up in the rented minibus. Eager for an adventure, we hopped on board. Excited chatter filled the ride to Kasylviv. Our kids anxiously anticipated seeing Andrii and Anna for the first time.

We arrived at the orphanage for our two-hour visit. Luda, the director's assistant, greeted us with her typical warmth. The young woman resembled actress Demi Moore with her long, dark hair and thin frame. She spoke little English but enough to convey kindness. Luda led us to a cramped room furnished with two small couches on opposite walls facing each other. A window at the far end, adorned with white lace curtains, allowed morning sunlight to filter in. On the left a door to a stark, dormitory-style bathroom with a drippy sink, two stalls and no toilet paper—I learned the hard way. Our four kids smooshed into the couch on the left. Wayne and I sat across from them.

Ten minutes later, Alexandra escorted Andrii and Anna into the room. She acted as translator and introduced them to their new siblings. I wondered if they felt like they walked into a lion's den. All business, Andrii nodded at his new brothers and sisters and shook their hands. Anna offered a timid smile and said a quick hello. Wayne pulled a blue Nerf football from his backpack. The squishy ball worked like a magnet drawing everyone together. I beamed as we took turns throwing the ball to each other—our first family activity.

Alex suggested we take the children outside. Bundled in coats and hats we headed into the chilly December air. A thin layer of frost sparkled on the carnival-colored swings, slide, monkey bars, teeter-totter, and balance beam, a direct contrast to Kasylviv's dreary landscape.

Six kids scattered across the playground. Andrii climbed and jumped on every piece of equipment. I couldn't wait to introduce him to Ezra—the neighbor boy back home about the same age and energy level. Anna preferred the swings and monkey bars. Missy and Sierra ran about trying to keep up with her. Wayne Jr. and Curtis tossed the blue football back and forth. My husband and Andrii played on the teeter-totter together. I roamed around snapping pictures proudly capturing the first images of our new family.

After an hour on the playground a worker poked her head out a window and beckoned to Andrii and Anna. We exchanged rushed waves and *pakas*, or good-byes, and watched the kids run back into the orphanage. Alex ushered us to the minibus. Gratitude and peace filled my heart on the ride back to Kyiv.

Our children, American and Ukrainian, had meshed well together. But little Sergey was missing. The kids hadn't met him yet. Wayne and I had only seen him twice.

Kasylviv required so much of our time and attention. Trips to Bryankiv only occurred when paperwork necessitated them. Visits with Sergey remained limited. I reassured myself that all seven children would soon be together. We would be a family of nine by Christmas. I hoped.

While Kasylviv orphanage staff welcomed us, one government official in the village did not. Alexandra referred to him as a man *like a mayor*. Though not an actual mayor, we needed his signature on our documents, which we discovered he wasn't planning to sign. Alex headed into Mayor Guy's office on December 4 while Wayne and I waited in the frigid car for more than an hour.

Though we wore winter coats and boots, we shivered in the backseat. Time dragged. Growing restless, we talked, prayed, read, napped, and nibbled on Ukrainian chocolate—necessary sustenance for adoption forays. Nothing seemed to keep our minds off the creeping sense of worry. What kept Alex so long? Our toes ached from the cold and our stomachs growled despite having snacks.

Wayne and I developed a strategy of not consuming much during these long days of orphanage visits and paperwork process-ing. Eating and drinking led to the need for a bathroom. Public restrooms were something we wanted to avoid, especially outside Kyiv. Beyond the city center, toilets were equivalent to holes in the floor. We dubbed them "squatty potties." The loathsome facilities were not on my list of things to do while in Ukraine.

An hour and a half later, Alexandra returned to the icy sardine can with news—Mayor Guy wouldn't be in his office for two more hours. She recommended passing the time at a nearby restaurant for lunch. There, we thawed out with crusty bread and savory borsht. I enjoyed the traditional beet and cabbage soup. Wayne preferred McDonald's or TGI Friday's back in Kyiv. My meat-and-potatoes hubby was not a fan of foreign food but braved the Ukrainian feast like a good sport. After lunch, I conquered my foe—the squatty potty.

Warm and fed, we resumed our backseat post, and Alexandra returned to Mayor Guy's office only to discover he'd already left for the day. His secretary recommended she try again tomorrow. We sat in silence on the ride back to Kyiv. Discouragement hung around our shoulders. We felt like prey in a cruel game of cat-and-mouse. A sick sport where children are the prize.

Early the next morning Wayne and I nestled again into the backseat of Stanislav's car. Our bag packed with clementines, a water bottle, and some Ukrainian chocolate. Apprehension pounded in my chest. I braced myself for another long day.

Alexandra announced she needed to gather documents in both Kasylviv and Bryankiv. Stanislav pointed his little car toward the closer village—Bryankiv.

Rummaging through her briefcase Alex said, "We have time this morning for you to visit Sergey." My spirits lifted at the unexpected news. Starting the day with our baby boy gave us a much-needed boost.

Wayne and I were again escorted to the upstairs playroom to wait for Sergey. Minutes later, the doctor brought him in. She reintroduced us as Mama and Papa. Our tiny, brown-eyed boy appeared shy—understandable for only our third visit.

I attempted to engage Sergey with the toys around us. He, more intrigued by Papa's glasses, gravitated toward Wayne who seized the opportunity to connect. Wayne reached down and put the glasses on the little guy's nose. We all laughed when Sergey played along making comical faces. He was just warming up to me when Alexandra entered with our documents in hand. Her arrival brought an abrupt end to our jovial visit. We waved goodbye to our boy and plodded back to the car.

The joy of the morning faded as we approached Kasylviv ninety minutes later. Stanislav parked on the street and turned off the engine. Again, Alexandra left us in the cold car and disappeared into a nearby office building. Her mission—a second attempt to obtain Mayor Guy's signature. The adoption could not move forward without signed documents.

Wayne and I prayed for Alex's success. Time dragged in the cold car. We chatted about the kids and nibbled on our usual snack: sweet clementines and Roshen chocolate. Stanislav grew restless too. He fiddled with his cell phone and radio and left the car a few times for a cigarette.

Two hours later, Alexandra returned with disappointing news. Mayor Guy never showed. She spoke with him by phone. He claimed he wouldn't be in the office for another six or seven days. My heart sank to my stomach. This village official avoided us on purpose, his stalling tactic an attempt to halt the adoption. Even with frozen toes and chattering teeth, I burned with frustration.

Somberness filled the ride back to Kyiv. I stared out the window. The dark Ukrainian countryside passed by. I prayed for God to intervene.

Alexandra whispered into the silence. "My government will soon shut down for the holidays. We are running out of time."

My heart dropped deeper into despair.

Traditional Ukrainian Christmas celebrations begin on December 24. Orthodox Christians observe the birth of Christ on January 7. Festivities end on January 19, the date of Epiphany. Wayne and I knew about the holiday timeline before we traveled for our November 29 appointment. With no major snafus, we should have enough time to complete an adoption and be home for Christmas.

Three weeks remained before the shutdown. I clenched my fists. We faced two choices: go home and return to Ukraine when the government reopened or stay and wait out the process. Going home seemed risky. Kasylviv officials could move Andrii and Anna to another orphanage. We might not find them when we returned. I squeezed my fists tighter, digging my fingernails into my palms. I refused to leave Ukraine without my children.

Navigating the adoption process was like climbing a rickety staircase to the unknown—each step a risk with no promise of survival. Wayne and I stood at the threshold and peered into darkness.

We still needed a court date to obtain an adoption decree. This appointment preceded a mandatory ten-day wait period. The wait provided an opportunity for anyone to contest the adoption. After ten days, a judge will sign the adoption decree and parents finally take custody of their children. Then they can apply for new birth certificates and passports. Once these documents are obtained, families finish the process at the American Embassy in Kyiv and fly home.

We were stuck on a step with a government official who refused to sign our documents. His opposition prohibited us from scheduling a court date—essentially blocking the adoption. I leaned back and folded my arms. Mayor Guy might hold the key to the next step, but I knew a strategy for unlocking doors.

CHAPTER 4

Weapons of Warfare

"What, then, shall we say in response to these things?
If God is for us, who can be against us?"

ROMANS 8:31 NIV

Though Wayne and I felt powerless against a foreign government, we had a secret weapon: prayer. James 5:16 (NLT) says, *"The earnest prayer of a righteous person has great power and produces wonderful results."* We needed results.

Together we made desperate pleas to the Lord. During our personal quiet times we urged God to move on our behalf. We reached out to our church family back home. Corporate prayer has been a powerful weapon. We didn't have internet in our apartment, so a few evenings each week I'd head to an internet café and email specific prayer requests to friends, family, and our church. Fervent petitions focused on securing Mayor Guy's signature. When the body of Christ comes together in prayer the power of God will be unleashed. Confident we were covered in prayer, we pressed on.

Alexandra called my cell on December 7. A new Mayor Guy in Kasylviv wanted to meet with us. Our interest piqued by the unusual request made by a new player. She left the decision up to us. A meeting with Mayor Guy number two might move things forward. Wayne and I recognized possible answered prayer. We looked at each other and nodded. "Yes, we agree to a meeting," I said.

Then, Alex delivered more news. She wouldn't be in town for the meeting. A different facilitator, Tonya, would accompany us. An unsettling blow. Though I'd only known her for two weeks, I recognized Alex as someone I wanted by my side. I felt my faith begin to fizzle as I hung up the phone.

The next morning, Tonya, a stunning dark-haired woman escorted us to Kasylviv. This time, instead of waiting in the car, Wayne and I entered the gray office building. My stomach felt like I'd ridden too many roller coasters. I checked my watch. Only 8:00 a.m.

In the waiting room a dozen chairs were arranged in a square. Tonya motioned for us to sit. Inspector Svetlana arrived. We exchanged brief smiles. At least one official in Kasylviv liked us. The two Ukrainian women exchanged a few words. Then, they gingerly entered an adjoining office to our right. Wayne and I remained alone in the waiting room. We sat in silence and prayed like crazy.

Fifteen minutes later Tonya and Inspector Svetlana emerged with some peculiar news. The first Mayor Guy had been fired. Two assistant mayors replaced him. One does not approve of foreigners adopting from Ukraine. The other, Victor, had requested the meeting. We would soon find out his view of adoption.

Mayor Victor agreed to see us at 9:00 a.m. None of us knew what this turn of events would bring. Wayne and I passed the time shifting in our seats and lifting up silent prayers.

At 9:30 a.m., a door to an office on our left opened. Tonya and Svetlana stood and motioned for us to follow them. Inside, Assistant Mayor Victor sat at a desk piled high with papers. He pointed to four empty chairs nearby.

Tonya acted as our interpreter while Victor asked us a series of questions: "Can you meet the children's medical needs? Do you live near a school? Do you have smoke alarms in your house? What religion are you? Will you bring the children to church? Do you bring your biological children to church?"

These questions both surprised and annoyed me. The children's needs he listed were barely, if at all, met in the orphanage.

Wayne and I smiled and answered the questions. Yes, we can meet their medical needs. Yes, we live near a school. Unsure how it might be received, we left out the homeschooling part. Yes, we have smoke detectors. We are Christian. We attend church as a family. Yes, yes, yes! Inside my head I screamed, "Are you kidding me? We can raise children a million times better than any government." On the outside, though, we sat like obedient dogs waiting for a treat.

Mayor Victor folded his hands and leaned forward. "I have a big responsibility to make a good decision for these children. I want God's will for them."

My heart quickened. We spoke the same language. Not English or Ukrainian, but the language of faith. I felt compelled to somehow show him adoption was God's will for these children.

I pulled a photo album out of my bag. Tonya handed the book to Victor and translated. The pictures featured our house, family, pets, swimming pool, and vehicles. Watching him flip the pages, I prayed his heart would be touched. He had to see a happy, loving family in the images. Victor's face showed zero emotion. I handed Tonya my next attempt to win the mayor's favor—Andrii's drawing.

Tonya unfolded and passed the artwork to Mayor Victor. During our second visit with the kids, Andrii had sketched a precious scene. On the right of the page he put a house with both a Ukrainian and American flag flying from the roof. On the other side he drew a smiling family of five—a dad wearing glasses, a curly-haired mom, and three happy children—a red-headed boy, a yellow-haired girl, and a tiny boy. I treasured the picture.

Victor scanned the drawing and put it aside. No emotion. The mayor thumbed through our documents. He turned his attention to Inspector Svetlana. They conversed in Ukrainian. Through tears she nodded and smiled and answered him. I felt certain she endorsed us.

Mayor Victor closed the file and told us to come back on Tuesday.

Tuesday? Tuesday was four days away. What about Monday? Why not sign our documents right now? The mayor stood. I guessed we were done. Inspector Svetlana and Tonya stood and motioned us to follow. Wayne and I smiled and offered the mayor our best *spa-cee-bah*, or thank you, and followed the women out the door.

We squeezed into our backseat for the ride back to Kyiv. A battle raged in my head—a fight between fear and faith. Fear fought to take over. The enemy of my soul wanted me to lose hope, give up, and go home.

Before the car left the parking lot, Romans 8:31 settled into my heart—*if God is for us, who can be against us?* Faith took root. God was for us. He was for kids. He was for family. And He was for adoption. Assistant Mayor Victor might be against us, but he was not more powerful than God.

With Alexandra out of town and no official adoption business to do, we scheduled a Saturday morning visit with Andrii and Anna. Wayne and I decided to bring our youngest biological kids along— Curtis and Sierra. Stanislav picked us up in a minibus, which puzzled me. We assumed he'd drive his car, so we left Wayne Jr. and Missy asleep in the apartment. Stan expected all four kids and brought the bigger vehicle. Ten rows of seats seemed extravagant compared to our cramped backseat.

We arrived at the orphanage at 10:00 a.m. Luda, the Demi Moore look-a-like, escorted us to the visitation room. Curtis and Sierra took their place on one couch. Wayne and I settled on the other. Moments later Andrii swaggered in. Anna strolled in behind him. They were at ease—visits with Mama and Papa now a regular treat for them. I reintroduced Curtis and Sierra. They exchanged hellos followed by awkward silence. The kids seemed unsure what to do next.

My mom instincts kicked in. I pulled paper and markers from my bag and passed them out. The four children drew silly pictures, each taking a turn holding theirs up. Laughter filled the small room.

Twenty minutes later a woman barged in and barked something at Andrii in Ukrainian. He ignored her and focused on his sketch. She repeated her demand with more sternness. Andrii capped his marker, abandoned his drawing, and left with her.

We were baffled by Andrii's abrupt exit but continued our visit with Anna. She colored for a short time, threw down her marker, and scooted out of the room. Wayne and I looked at each other not sure what to make of her disappearance. Two minutes later Anna marched in like the Pied Piper with four kids behind her.

The children, curious about the American visitors, smiled sheepishly. I handed them cookies, which they gobbled up. The kids giggled at my attempt to speak Russian with them. Anna, the center of attention, reveled in the impromptu party. Curtis and Sierra passed around paper and markers.

One boy, about eight years old, ran out of the room. Moments later he returned and handed me a sketchbook. I smiled and nodded my approval at each drawing. He beamed every time I said *doh-bray*, or good. The young artist proudly gifted me some of his treasured sketches.

Two hours later, most of the children had dispersed to other parts of the orphanage. We were enjoying our remaining minutes with Anna when Stanislav returned to pick us up. He walked into the room, and I shook my head, shrugged, and said, "No Andrii?" He understood my question and went to investigate.

Wayne pulled the Nerf football out of his coat pocket and threw it to Curtis who tossed it to Anna who lobbed it at Sierra. We laughed and enjoyed the game. My heart swelled with pride. Curtis and Sierra made a genuine effort to include Anna. Pitch-and-catch helped our family interact.

It also passed the time while we waited for Stanislav. He came back thirty minutes later and handed me his cell phone. Confused, I held the phone to my ear. I heard Alexandra's voice on the other end. She explained the mystery of our son's disappearance—the orphanage worker had taken Andrii to buy him new clothes. I thanked Alex and handed Stan his phone. Wayne shot me a puzzled look. I rolled my eyes.

The children's clothes belonged to the orphanage like community property. When Andrii and Anna leave, their wardrobe stays. I knew we needed to provide every piece of clothing from underwear and socks to coats and hats. We missed an important family visit with Andrii for an absurd reason.

I grabbed my coat and marched myself out to the minibus— resisting the urge to stomp my feet the entire way. Kasylviv made me want to scream.

Back in Kyiv later that afternoon, we hunkered down with Wayne Jr., Missy, Curtis, and Sierra. In our pajamas, we sprawled on the futon together, watched DVDs, and munched on snacks. The kids needed our attention. Most of their time was spent in the apartment. They slept the day away while Wayne and I were off doing adoption business. Our family craved some normalcy. A typical weekend back home included visiting friends and attending church on Sunday—we all had a desperate need for both. I grabbed the cell phone and called my friend, Laura.

Joey and Laura Stoltzfus served as an anchor for our family during the adoption. Laura's parents, Stan and Mary Slager, pastored our church back home. Joey and Laura were missionaries on the Youth With A Mission (YWAM) base in Kyiv. The Stoltzfus's extended boundless hospitality and friendship to us throughout our time in Ukraine. They blessed us with home cooked meals, tours of the city, holiday activities, and rides to church.

Laura and I made plans for our two families to spend Sunday, December 10, together. The next morning, Joey, Laura and their three young children picked us up for church. Our family of six squeezed into the Stoltzfus's minivan. We headed to International Church Assembly—an Assemblies of God church filled with expats and missionaries.

The service, conducted in English, ministered to my parched soul. I soaked up the Scripture reading from Colossians 1:9-12 about bearing fruit in every good work. Verse 11 in the NIV resonated with me, "being strengthened with all power according to his glorious might so that you may have great endurance and patience." I scribbled the verse in my journal. Strength, endurance, and patience—all needed for the journey ahead.

After church our families gathered at the Stolzfus's apartment for lunch and fellowship. Laura cooked eggs and pancakes, and brewed Dunkin Donuts coffee we'd brought from the states. The tastes and smells of home wrapped around me like a hug.

We relished conversation with our American friends. For two weeks the only English we heard came from our own mouths or Alexandra's—hers spoken with a beautiful Ukrainian accent. We spent so much time with Alex, I found myself speaking English with a Ukrainian accent.

Before we left the Stoltzfus's apartment I used their internet. The seven-hour time difference meant our church in New York would be gathering for Sunday morning worship in just a few hours. I seated myself at their computer, and like a soldier on a top-secret mission, I emailed prayer requests to our church family—highlighting Mayor Victor's signature as top priority. Each email sent bolstered my faith. In a matter of hours an entire congregation would cover us in prayer.

Early Monday morning my cell phone rang. With Alexandra away we assumed we had a day off and planned to sleep in. Groggy and confused by who might be calling, I reached for the phone. "Good morning, we will be there in fifteen minutes to pick you up."

Alex, in Kyiv and back at work. The announcement jarred me awake. Without argument I hung up the phone. Wayne and I threw on our warmest clothing, grabbed our coats, and rushed out the door.

We slid into our backseat post. Alexandra explained she wanted to see the judge in Bryankiv. With the process stalled in Kasylviv, maybe we could at least obtain a court date for Sergey's adoption. Wayne and I trusted savvy Alexandra. She did the paperwork, met with government officials, and hustled the adoption along. We believed we were in good hands. Even if she did leave us in a cold car for hours each day.

Snow flurries filled the air as we pulled into Bryankiv. Alexandra stepped out of the car and disappeared into a nearby cement office building, gray and drab like all the others on the street. The coating of white made me think of Christmas—only two weeks away. I tried pushing the thoughts out of my head. Worry about the adoption's impact on the holiday messed with my faith. Would we be home for Christmas? Would the adoption be finalized? What about our biological kids? What about our Ukrainian kids? Alex's return to the car thirty minutes later rescued me from my torment.

She brushed the snowflakes from her coat and sighed. Our staunch facilitator sat with a pile of documents on her lap. She folded her hands and looked at us in the backseat from the mirror on her sun visor. "The judge does not want to give us a court date without the Mayor's signature from Kasylviv."

Alexandra had worked every angle. To save time she hoped to schedule one court hearing with one judge for all three children. If that didn't work, then two court dates were required—one in Bryankiv and one in Kasylviv. Scheduling two hearings with two different judges would drag out the process even longer. However, without the elusive signature none could be scheduled. Alex sat up straight, inhaled deeply, and announced, "Now we go to Kasylviv."

Stanislav and Alexandra dropped Wayne and I off at the orphanage. We watched them speed away—straight to Mayor Victor's office. Our determined facilitator was not about to wait until Tuesday for his signature. While grateful for more time with Andrii and Anna, we found focusing difficult. Our minds were on Alex and her mission.

We enjoyed our visit, but the hands on the clock barely moved. Andrii showed off his handy-man skills. He hooked up an old computer and drew a picture of a family on the screen. Anna soaked up attention by doing gymnastics tricks for us. She stood on her head. We clapped. She performed a backbend. We applauded. For the first time, she asked me to pick her up. Of course, I obliged and my heart swelled. With growling stomachs, Wayne and I shared our stash of clementines and chocolate with our kids, who loved Mama and Papa's lunch.

Other orphan children wandered into the visitation room. They initiated a game of hide-and-seek, which spilled into a main living area. Some of the boys dragged in a life-size stuffed tiger. Their eyes gleamed when they held up toy hunting knives. I played photographer while each child posed with the prized animal. They beamed when they saw themselves on the camera's digital screen.

The children dispersed when called to dinner an hour later. Luda, our Demi Moore friend, invited Wayne and I to eat. We declined. Taking food meant for orphans didn't seem right to us. While the kids were eating, I checked the time. Four o'clock. We'd never been at the orphanage this late before.

I started to think Alexandra had forgotten us. Moments later she strolled into the visitation room. Our devoted facilitator hugged me and said, "Congratulations." The salutation confused me. With a look of satisfaction on her face, she clarified, "I got the signature."

In that moment, warmth radiated through me. I knew the prayers lifted up by our church family back home were answered.

We stood in the visitation room and listened while Alex explained her confrontation with Mayor Victor. "First I waited in his office for two hours. Then, I fought with him for three hours. This man does not approve of adoption. He said he would not sign our documents on Tuesday or any day."

Riveted by her story, I tried to process the meaning of Alex's words while she continued, "I informed him, if he does not sign, I will call the main prosecutor in Kyiv. He would have to answer to a judge. This would be inconvenient for him."

The mayor became angry and made a call. After discovering Alexandra's tactic wasn't an empty threat but part of the legal process, he slammed down the phone. The mayor signed the documents and ordered Alex out of his office.

My heart soared all the way back to Kyiv. I marveled at how God positioned Alexandra as our facilitator. She went to bat for us when most would have given up. Her unwavering commitment to adoption and love for children fueled her fight. She secured the signature, which enabled the adoption to move forward. I drifted off to sleep that night content both God and Alex were on our side.

The ordeal with the mayor had cost us two weeks. The lost time led to another endurance test—three children wanted to go home. With Christmas fourteen days away, Wayne Jr., Curtis, and Sierra missed their friends and family. Wayne and I understood their longing. I missed my life back in New York too. My routine, my coffee, my bed, my bathroom, my mom. The pending holiday made it hard on us all, especially the kids. As much as I wanted them with me, it didn't seem fair to make them stay. We conceded and booked their return flights.

Our sixteen-year-old daughter, Melissa, chose to remain in Ukraine with us. Missy had been on a mission trip with me back in 2004. She'd grown to love Ukraine and wanted to stay as long as possible.

Three days later I awoke with an aching heart. I helped the kids pack and choked back salty tears when Sierra curled up on Wayne's lap. The sight of father and daughter cuddled together wrecked me. I ran to the bathroom for the third time that morning.

Before leaving for the airport, Wayne gathered our somber family into a circle. We joined hands as he prayed over our children. I sobbed. My babies were about to board an international flight and fly through the night across the Atlantic Ocean alone. I hated the thought of it. Two anxious grandmothers to receive them at JFK was my only consolation.

Wayne instructed Wayne Jr. and Curtis to stay together and keep their little sister close. I wrapped my arms around each precious kid not sure when I would see them again. I knew we would not be together for Christmas. When the door closed behind them, I ran to the bathroom again.

While Wayne and Joey Stoltzfus drove the kids to the airport, Missy helped me pack up our things. With only three of us, the expensive flat was no longer necessary. We planned to move into a smaller apartment on Rusonifka, an island-like suburb of Kyiv. The move also put us walking distance from the Stoltzfus's, which would prove a huge benefit in the coming weeks.

I zipped up the last suitcase when Tonya called to report she'd delivered our documents to the courthouse in Kasylviv for Alexandra. My spirit perked up when she said the judge agreed to combine both court cases for the adoption. We first thought it would take two separate hearings, one in Kasylviv and one in Bryankiv. Court for all three children together simplified the process. Simpler meant faster, I calculated. This news lifted my mood for about two seconds—until Tonya said, "The judge cannot take the case until December 26."

A court date in late December would keep us in Ukraine until the end of January. The mandatory ten-day waiting period begins the day after court. If the date were December 26, ours would last until the second week in January. We could not take Andrii, Anna, or Sergey from the orphanage until the wait ended and the judge signed the court decree. At that point the government would be shut down for the holidays. My biological kids felt farther away than ever. My Ukrainian children didn't feel much closer.

Wayne and Joey returned for Missy and me. We loaded our luggage into the Stoltzfus's silver minivan—a vehicle with New York license plates, an oddity in Kyiv. Joey had the van shipped from the United States. Their family of five needed a car bigger than a sardine can.

No one said much on the thirty-minute drive to Rusonifka, which was fine with me. I didn't feel like talking. I wanted to be home driving my SUV with New York plates. I wanted my kids, all seven of them together with me and Wayne under one roof.

Our new apartment did not help my mood. It felt like we moved from a Manhattan high-rise to a Brooklyn tenement. Inside they were cold and dated. Our apartment had one bedroom for Wayne and me. Missy claimed the couch, happy to be in familiar territory. Rusonifka was the same community we stayed in on our mission trip two years earlier. We knew how to get to the grocery store and the YWAM base, both just a few blocks away.

Though clean the entire place skeeved me out. Our new home lacked a washing machine. We now had to hand wash our clothes and hang them around the apartment to dry. The bathroom seemed a strange setup to us Americans with the tub and sink in one room and the toilet in a separate closet-side room. Our kitchen looked like a throw-back to the 1960s. It didn't matter. Most days I only had time to boil water for tea and instant soup. But it was less expensive than the Kyiv apartment. And only a six-minute walk to Joey and Laura's. We unpacked and settled in—the entire time my mind on my babies in the sky somewhere over the Atlantic.

In the midst of the gloom Tonya called again. I braced myself for more bad news.

"I must go to Bryankiv to pick up Sergey's documents," she said. "Would you like to go along and visit him?"

My despondent heart fluttered. Time with three-year-old Sergey would provide much needed nourishment for my weary soul.

On our way to Bryankiv, Tonya called the orphanage to inform them of our visit. She was told Sergey had been hospitalized for bronchitis. The news snapped me out of my gloom. My baby was sick and needed me. I demanded Tonya take us to the hospital.

After going through proper channels, Tonya obtained permission for us to visit Sergey. He was in the small medical center down the street from the orphanage. An hour later, Wayne and I held hands as we entered the stark, cement building. With each step I silently prayed for Sergey to not be seriously ill.

When we arrived, a nurse informed us that Sergey was asleep. We were directed to wait in a room adjacent to the children's ward. The stench of kerosene floated in as a man painted walls in a nearby stairwell.

A uniformed hospital worker entered the waiting room. My eyes nearly bugged out of my head as I watched her slosh a rag around in a bucket of dirty water, ring it out with her bare hands, drop it on the floor, and push it around with a broomstick. She repeated the "cleaning" process a half-dozen times. I wanted to scream, "Isn't this a hospital? Don't you know about germs?" Instead, I leaned my head against the wall, closed my eyes, and prayed I'd never need to be hospitalized in Ukraine.

Thirty minutes later a nurse directed us to Sergey's room. Dressed in pink sweatpants and a blue sweatshirt, our boy looked pale but alert. He acted shy again until I brought out cookies and a juice box. After a quick lesson on how to drink from a straw, he devoured the snack. The little guy perked up when Wayne pulled a Matchbox car from his coat pocket. He giggled and coughed as we pushed the toy back and forth on a small table beside his bed. I reveled in the moment knowing this precious boy will soon be my son.

After only twenty minutes a different nurse barged in, babbled something in Ukrainian, waved her hands, and swooshed us out of the room. Tonya translated, "It's time for Sergey to sleep." Wayne and I waved goodbye over our shoulders. While grateful he didn't appear gravely sick, I couldn't wait to get him home where I could care for him myself.

On our way back to the apartment Tonya told us to be ready early the next morning. She needed to give Sergey's documents to the judge in Kasylviv. And she planned to ask the judge for an earlier court date.

Do I dare to hope for such a thing? My head pounded. Not sure if it was from the day's events, the kerosene smell, or the cold I felt coming on. I felt lousy.

Before bed, Wayne and I prayed together—the only action we could take—for our kids still on their flight home, Sergey in the hospital, Andrii and Anna, and the court date. I learned when we are in our comfort zone at home, we tend to do a lot of things in our own strength. At least I do. There are resources to utilize, people to talk to, and options to try. But in Ukraine, Wayne and I only had each other and the Lord. Our faith grew as we became more dependent on Him. I took comfort in Romans 8:28 (NIV) "And we know that in all things God works for the good of those who love him, who have been called according to his purpose." We loved God and He called us to this adoption. I decided to trust Him to work it all out.

My cell phone rang around 3:00 a.m. I pounced. My mom's voice crackled on the other end. "We have the kids. They're safe." I thanked her and God. Laying my head back on the pillow I cried myself to sleep.

The next day the judge in Kasylviv scheduled court for Tuesday, December 19—just four days away. God did indeed work all things together for good. It felt like a miracle.

Later that evening, I spent some time thanking God and meditating on His Word. Wrapped in my fleece blanket from home,

I curled up with a hot cup of black tea and opened my Bible. With Christmas only one week away, I opened to the Gospel of Luke in my Parallel Bible. Luke 1:37 in the New King James Version resonated with me: "For with God nothing will be impossible." Snuggled in warmth, I held onto that truth and fell asleep.

On Friday, we enjoyed a day off while Tonya shuffled our documents between Bryankiv and Kasylviv in preparation for court. We called home and talked with Wayne Jr., Curtis, and Sierra. They sounded well and happy to be home. Hearing their voices brought me some relief, but I still missed them. And I didn't dare let myself think about Christmas.

Wayne, Missy, and I planned to relax over the weekend. We spent Saturday playing countless rounds of Yahtzee, drinking bottomless cups of hot tea, and emailing prayer requests to friends and family back home.

The next day, we again joined Joey and Laura for church. The Sunday School children performed a quaint little Christmas program. The pastor preached from Luke 1. He pointed out Mary's obedience to God's will. My faith strengthened as I recognized God speaking to me through the Scriptures. I relished the Christmas themed service until the hymn *"O Holy Night."* Tears streamed down my cheeks through the entire song. My weary soul longed to rejoice and craved the thrill of hope.

Monday marked three weeks in Ukraine. To celebrate, Wayne and I spent the entire day in the backseat of Stanislav's car. Both Alexandra and Tonya hustled us and our documents between Kyiv, Bryankiv, and Kasylviv. We bounced back and forth like a ping-pong ball. Sometimes our signatures were needed. Most of the time we sat in the cold, waiting and praying.

On Tuesday, December 19, 2006, our long-anticipated court date arrived. We waited in the stark courthouse lobby for our appointment with the judge. My body shook from nervousness or cold or both. Even Alexandra seemed anxious. She informed us the assistant director of Andrii and Anna's orphanage would join us. When Luda walked in, I was surprised. We didn't know our kind friend held such an important position. Inspector Svetlana and the Inspector from Bryankiv, whom we'd never met, also came in. Our legal team stood together exchanging an occasional whisper.

Weary from standing, I lowered myself onto the edge of a wooden bench. I sat in silent prayer. My heart raced. The entire adoption and future of our Ukrainian children depended on what happened next.

Wayne and I entered an immense courtroom adorned in polished wood. The vast size made me feel like a tiny bug about to be squashed. I stared at the metal cage to the left of the judge's bench. My mind waffled between faith and fear while my stomach flip-flopped.

The judge entered and her appearance amazed me. I had not expected a beautiful, blonde-haired woman in her forties. She reminded me of Patty Blake, a woman back home with a vibrant personality. The sight of her helped disarm my fear—a little.

Two prosecutors dressed in black flanked the judge. The man on her left wore a sour expression. He was from the mayor's office in Kasylviv. I tried to avoid looking at him or the metal cage.

The judge read our adoption application out loud. Alexandra stood behind us and translated in whispered tones. The document stated Wayne and Sandra Flach wanted to adopt the three children and become their parents and included a request to change their names and permission to apply for new birth certificates.

The judge asked us to stand and state our names and birthdates. She asked us questions such as: "Why do you want to adopt from

Ukraine?" "When did you meet these children?" "Do they like you?" "What will your other kids think of them?" "Do you have a big enough house?" "Enough money?" "Does your home have smoke detectors?" "Can you meet their medical needs?" We answered each question in a respectful manner.

The prosecutor on the right said nothing. The man from the mayor's office asked one question, "What does your family at home think of you adopting these children?" Alex translated our answer, "Our family back home already considers these children ours."

The two inspectors and the assistant director of the orphanage each spoke in favor of the adoption. The judge seemed satisfied. She said we could pick up the final adoption decree in ten days. Since the tenth day would be a Saturday, Alexandra asked if we could pick up the court decree one day early on December 29. Our judge agreed. She also allowed Saturdays and Sundays to be counted as part of the ten days. The gavel slammed down. I released a deep exhale.

The countdown to bring our kids home had begun.

CHAPTER 5

Adoption is Costly

"The sacrifice you desire is a broken spirit. You will not reject a broken and repentant heart, O God."

PSALM 51:17 NLT

A doption comes with a price—and not just in monetary terms. For me, part of the cost included six weeks in Ukraine and Christmas without my family. Our children, though, were worth the sacrifice, but payment can be painful.

I never saw the Christmas tree, which stood in my house that December of 2006. Wayne Jr. and Curtis took advantage of our absence and chose the largest tree on the lot. Their little sister, Sierra, adorned it with our family decorations. My parents accompanied the kids to our annual Flach family Christmas Eve celebration. We called Wayne's brother's house during the festivities. I choked back tears while we talked with our kids, our parents, and other family members.

My parents stayed overnight at our house so the kids wouldn't wake up alone on Christmas morning. Before we traveled to Ukraine, I had purchased and put away a few gifts for each of them. At least they would have some presents to open. I instructed my mom on what to do for stocking stuffers. She even made the kids Christmas breakfast and dinner, but still I knew this holiday paled in comparison to our traditional Christmases. For the first time in their lives Wayne Jr., Curtis, and Sierra would not wake up to my special quiche, a mountain of gifts, or their parents. It was also the first time I missed a Christmas with my mom. I hated feeling like I ruined everyone's holiday.

On Christmas day, Wayne, Missy, and I walked through light falling snow to the Stoltzfus's apartment. Laura served us coffee and homemade cinnamon rolls. I fought back tears as we watched their three children open gifts. How I longed to be home watching my own kids unwrapping presents.

Later that day we joined Joey and Laura for the YWAM base Christmas party. We enjoyed a program and dinner with about 100 YWAM staff. I felt a camaraderie with all those missionaries. Most of them were far away from home and family as well. I forced myself through the celebration with a smile. Inside I just wanted the day to be over.

My head hit the pillow that night thankful Ukraine time is seven hours ahead of New York. With Christmas behind us, we could now focus on bringing our children home. Before turning off the light, I opened my Bible. Isaiah 40:4-5 in the New Living Translation drew me in: "Fill in the valleys, and level the mountains and hills. Straighten the curves, and smooth out the rough places. Then the glory of the Lord will be revealed, and all people will see it together. The Lord has spoken." I read further in Isaiah 40:10-11:

> "Yes, the Sovereign Lord is coming in power. He will rule with a powerful arm. See, He brings his reward with Him as He comes. He will feed His flock like a shepherd. He will carry the lambs in His arms, holding them close to His heart. He will gently lead the mother sheep with their young."

God spoke to me through these verses. He called us to this adoption and would straighten our path. By His powerful right arm, He would lead this mama home with her young. I drifted off to sleep comforted by truth—my God would accomplish all He purposed.

The day after Christmas brought another difficult test—saying goodbye to Wayne. We reached a point in the adoption process where he could return home. I clung to my husband and cried. The children at home, his job, and the addition being built onto our house all needed his attention. Though I was happy our kids would have their dad back, waves of envy and apprehension pounded my heart. Wayne would get to hug our children, sleep in our bed, and enjoy the comforts of home while Missy and I remained in Ukraine without him.

After one last kiss goodbye, Wayne walked out the door. I turned the locks and wiped my tears. A fierce resolve welled up inside me. I would put on my big girl boots and finish the process without him. I would bring Andrii, Anna, and Sergey home.

CHAPTER 6

Getting our Kids

"Now all glory to God, who is able, through his mighty power at work within us, to accomplish infinitely more than we might ask or think."

EPHESIANS 3:20 NLT

The day after Wayne left, Missy and I enjoyed two hours of fun with Sergey at the orphanage. Out of the hospital but still congested, he let me hold him much of the visit. The tiny guy devoured two whole bananas, a juice box, fruit snacks, and a cookie. While he sat on my lap, he sucked both middle and index finger on his right hand. At one point he hopped down and stuck his feet in Missy's winter boots. We laughed as he trudged around the room acting silly. I treasured every moment with my new little son.

Alexandra stood in the doorway and motioned for Missy and me to come. I sighed. Three days remained of the ten-day wait. I yearned to bring my baby boy home. For now, I waved goodbye and walked out the door.

After the visit, Stanislav dropped Missy and I off at the Stolzfus's apartment. We savored Laura's home-cooked beef stew and biscuits. While I relaxed on their couch with a cup of hot coffee, my cell phone rang. Alexandra called with news that stunned me. "I spoke with the orphanage director in Kasylviv. Your ten-day wait ends on Saturday, December 30. We cannot pick up the children on a holiday weekend. The director was nice. She has given us permission to pick up Andrii and Anna—tomorrow."

"What? Tomorrow?" I wasn't sure I understood. After all the waiting, getting the children early didn't seem possible.

"Yes, tomorrow," Alex repeated.

A combination of excitement and panic pulsed through me. In less than twenty-four hours I would have two of our kids with me. This unexpected blessing would lead to an interesting excursion to Kasylviv for me later on. But for now, my heart rejoiced in God's favor.

The sudden turn of events caught me off-guard. Ill prepared to pick up the kids so soon, I hadn't even gotten clothes for them yet. In a frenzy, Laura and I threw on our coats and ran down to a small, corner store in the neighborhood. Thirty minutes before closing we grabbed underwear, socks, jeans, and shirts. Laura threw coats, hats, gloves, and winter boots onto the pile. She helped me guess sizes for all three kids. We left with four bags stuffed with clothes. Not an extensive wardrobe, but enough until I got them home.

The next morning my spirit soared all the way to Kasylviv. When we arrived at the orphanage all the children buzzed with excitement. A holiday production much like a school program back home was about to begin. The director invited Alexandra and me to stay for the special presentation. We could leave with the children afterward. Declining her invitation didn't seem like an option, so we followed her to a large all-purpose room.

Chairs lined one end of the hall. A Christmas tree stood on a platform at the other. The old wooden floor in between remained empty. The director motioned for us to take our seats with about thirty other people. I looked around, enthralled by the festive atmosphere. Sparkling decorations adorned cement walls—a stark contrast compared to the typical dreariness of orphanage life.

Alex leaned over and whispered, "The mayor is in the audience. We are not supposed to be here."

Her words hit like a sucker punch. I realized my mere presence at a Christmas program could jeopardize the adoption.

A sudden noise drew my attention to the doorway. Giggling, singing children of various ages marched into the room, each child dressed for the occasion. The younger ones were either in formal attire or animal costumes. The older teenage girls wore vyshyvanka, traditional Ukrainian embroidered dresses.

Like a proud mama I searched for my children in the crowd. I spotted Andrii first. He donned a chicken costume. My little Anna floated into the room like a princess in a powder-blue floor-length dress. To my amazement, she found me in the audience, took my hand, and led me to the center of the room.

Familiar sounding music started to play. I found myself in a circle of orphans doing the Chicken Dance. Over the months of waiting I dreamed often about our adoption. Not once did my dreams include me dancing the Chicken Dance.

As music and laughter filled the air, my fear of grumpy government officials disappeared. This mama pulled off the "quack-quack, waddle-waddle" dance moves much to Anna's delight. I relished the experience knowing this was the last day my children would be orphans.

After the program Andrii and Anna changed into the clothes I'd bought them. Andrii strutted into the room pleased with his new blue jeans and Anna twirled about in her puffy pink coat. I clapped and rubbed my hands together, relieved to have scored a mom-win with my fashion choices.

I sensed the palpable emotions of the staff and older orphans. Some cried while we took pictures and said goodbye. A teenage girl called Anna over to sit on her lap. She cried and hugged her, and Anna seemed oblivious. A woman, the kids' primary caregiver, ran out to the car as we piled in. She sobbed and waved as we pulled away from the orphanage. Andrii and Anna never shed a tear. They looked forward to the adventure ahead. I wondered how much they understood.

Twice on the ride back to Kyiv we stopped on the side of the road because Andrii got car sick. I rubbed his back while he threw up and marveled at his bravery. He and Anna left everything behind to go with me into the unknown.

We got to the apartment around 6:00 p.m. Andrii and Anna flew out of the car and into the building. Even though they had no idea where to go, they scrambled up two flights of stairs ahead of me. Laughing at their exuberance, I pointed to our door. I dug the key out of my coat pocket while the kids bounced around waiting for me to let them in. Our happy party spilled into the apartment. We hadn't even taken off our coats when Laura and Missy arrived with a pot of soup, groceries, and my friend—Jocelyn Heneghan.

When Wayne returned home, we realized Missy and I would need help with the three kids. We asked Jocelyn to fly over and assist us. She had led several mission trips for our church, including the one Missy and I took to Ukraine back in 2004. Jocelyn, in her late twenties, also was the oldest of ten kids and a youth group leader. She possessed the necessary skills to manage our menagerie.

Laura, fluent in Russian, introduced herself and Jocelyn to Andrii and Anna. After Laura left, we devoured bowls of hot soup and hunks of buttered bread. Andrii and Anna took turns soaking in long, hot bubble baths. They ate dinner again and gobbled up chips, cookies, and juice boxes. When I realized we would soon run out of food at the pace the kids were eating, I closed the kitchen for the night.

The five of us settled in for the evening. Missy entertained the kids with her Game Boy. The three of them cuddled up on the couch with the electronic gadget. Jocelyn and I exchanged news. She filled me in on events back home and I updated her on the adoption. I fell asleep with an almost full heart. Two of our three children slept nearby. Tomorrow would be Sergey's turn to leave the orphanage behind.

CHAPTER 7

And Then
There Were Four

*"Trust in the LORD with all your heart and lean not on your
own understanding; In all your ways submit to him and he
will make your paths straight."*

Proverbs 3:5-6 NIV

F riday morning, December 29, I left Andrii and Anna in the
capable hands of Jocelyn and Missy. Alexandra and Tonya
picked me up at 7:00 a.m. The women had an agenda—get the
kids' new birth certificates so we could apply for their passports and
pick up Sergey. First, we headed for Kasylviv to obtain the court
decree. I used the long ride as an opportunity to ask Alex a question
that nagged me, "How would we know if the children had other
siblings?"

The question made sense to me because all three kids had the
same biological mother and father listed on their Ukrainian birth
certificates. Court documents also revealed that in 2002, when
Andrii was five and Anna three, they were found alone in a shack
without food or heat. Authorities took the abandoned children
to the orphanage. Parental rights were eventually terminated by a
judge, and they became orphans with living parents.

In 2003, their mother gave birth to Sergey. She abandoned him at the hospital. A short time later he was moved to the baby house in Bryankiv. Parental rights to him were terminated as well. The kids were now nine, seven, and three years old. From the court records I calculated the birth mom to be about twenty-seven. Young enough to have more children.

After an awkward pause, Alexandra looked at me through the mirror in the sun visor, as she often did while I sat in my backseat perch. Her blue eyes were serious, her answer almost an apology, "We just found out. I was not sure how to tell you. There is a fourth sibling."

I grasped the headrest, thrusted myself forward, and peppered Alex with questions: How old? Boy or girl? Where? She didn't know the answers but promised to find out. My heartbeat accelerated and my mind spun. A fourth child? I had no idea how to process this news. The rest of the ride to Kasylviv I prayed for God's guidance while Alex made calls from her cell phone.

In Kasylviv, Alexandra left me in the car and disappeared into the courthouse. Her quick return surprised me. She had the document, but it was post-dated December 30. This detail meant we couldn't apply for the kids' new birth certificates until Monday. It also held up the application process for the passports. I felt the heat of the holiday shutdown on my neck. Frustrated by another setback, we headed for Bryankiv.

My mind reeled while the car sped toward the unknown. While excited to get Sergey, I worried about the kids in the apartment. How were Jocelyn and Missy doing with Andrii and Anna? What about this potential fourth child? Will we ever get the birth certificates and passports? How do I navigate all of this without Wayne? My entire being screamed to get off this roller coaster ride. I wanted my three children and I wanted to go home. To stop the surge of emotions I turned to God—my only solace and source of survival.

By the time we pulled up to the orphanage in Bryankiv, Alex's phone calls had yielded some answers. The children's birth mother had another baby boy in 2005. She abandoned him at the hospital just as she had done with Sergey two years prior. The infant named Slava, now fourteen months old, has been in the baby house in Bryankiv ever since.

I attempted to digest the details. This child has been here in the orphanage with Sergey all along? All those times we visited and never knew he existed. Why hadn't anyone revealed this important information sooner?

Alexandra tried to explain. "The baby's documents are not in order. Parental rights have not been terminated. He was abandoned at birth but is not yet legally available for adoption."

My heart broke for this little boy. Though I only learned of his existence a few hours earlier, I sensed he belonged with us too. I asked Alex if we could see him before leaving the orphanage. She nodded and promised, "I will try."

Inside the orphanage Alexandra and I waited in the unheated lobby area. A worker came by and took the clothes I brought for Sergey. She babbled something in Russian and darted up the stairs, her slippers silent on the tile floor. Alex translated, "The worker said Sergey would be more comfortable if she changed him into his new clothes."

A reasonable point. Not that I had a choice. The woman and the clothing were already gone.

Alexandra escorted me to an upstairs office so I could complete the necessary paperwork while she went in search of the orphanage director. Inside the small office, the doctor in her white lab coat sat at a neat and tidy desk. She offered me the chair beside her. I sat. She opened a folder and handed me a pen. The doctor pointed to a line and I signed my name. She closed the folder and stood. That was it. No emotional goodbye. No tears shed. It felt like we'd just conducted a business transaction—like I'd just purchased a car.

The worker who'd taken Sergey's clothes delivered him to the office and left. The little boy looked smaller than ever dressed in his over-sized denim overalls and red winter coat. Laura and I had guessed his size to be much bigger than he actually was.

Captivated by his cuteness, I smiled and reached out. Sergey put his tiny hand in mine. Together we followed the doctor downstairs.

Alexandra waited for us at the bottom step. She and the doctor spoke in Russian. After their conversation, the doctor escorted us through the lobby, past the exit, and to a hallway I hadn't gone down before. She paused by a Dutch door. No one said a word, but I knew what was about to happen.

The doctor motioned for us to stay in the hall while she entered the room. Moments later the top door opened, and the doctor held up a young child clothed in yellow-footed pajamas.

Little Slava appeared much smaller than fourteen months old. Green, crossed eyes peeked out from under the baby bonnet tied below his chin. Mesmerized I reached through the doorway and touched his hand. "Lord, what about this child?"

Sensing the brevity of the moment, I waved and said, "Paka," meaning bye-bye. Sergey mimicked me and waved also. Both boys were too young to understand the poignant situation. They didn't even know they were brothers.

Seconds later, Alex touched my arm. Time to go. We made our way out to the car. Little Sergey in his red coat held my hand. Tiny Slava in the yellow pajamas held a piece of my heart.

In the car I put Sergey on my lap and tried to sort out the day's events. But I didn't have time to dwell on Slava. My busy boy kept me distracted on the ride back to our apartment. It appeared to be his first ride in a *machina*. He climbed all over the backseat trying to look out every window. The little guy kept reaching for the door handle. I kept one hand on him at all times and made a mental note—tell Wayne to purchase a car seat.

My frazzled nerves relaxed when we finally pulled up to our apartment building forty minutes later. I slid out of the car, placed little Sergey on the ground, and took his hand. We waved paka to the machina as Alexandra drove away.

After the car disappeared down the street, I turned to enter the building. Sergey squatted and cried. Attempts to coax him failed. He refused to hold my hand. The scared little boy would not budge. Desperate to get him inside before someone called the police, I scooped him into my arms and carried him up two flights of stairs. Both of us crying every step of the way.

My heart broke for Sergey. A woman he barely knew, who didn't speak his language, carried him into a strange building. Everyone and everything familiar to him now gone. He feared the unknown. No wonder my attempts to hush and comfort him failed.

Moments later we reached the apartment door. I knocked. While Jocelyn fiddled with the lock, I could hear commotion inside. She opened the door to reveal an ecstatic Andrii and Anna jumping up and down. Their excitement flipped a switch in Sergey. He stopped crying, and I put him down. He joined the kids laughing and dancing around the apartment. The siblings were still strangers, but the fun defused his fear.

My empathy turned to joy. Jocelyn, Missy, and I watched Andrii, Anna, and Sergey together for the first time. At that moment the siblings did not know about little Slava back in Bryankiv—and neither did my husband.

After we got the kids fed and settled, I called home. Wayne, amazed to hear we finally had all three kids, kept saying, "Wow!" Then I told him we didn't have the full set. My discovery of Slava tumbled out. We discussed our options and agreed our hands were full with Andrii, Anna, and Sergey. Slava was not even available for adoption yet. Wayne and I decided to keep him in our hearts and trust God to guide the way. We chose to not tell anyone else about Slava until the Lord opened that door.

CHAPTER 8

Entertaining Angels

"But thanks be to God! He gives us the victory
through our Lord Jesus Christ."

1 CORINTHIANS 15:57 NIV

January loomed only days away. Although I had the kids, I didn't have all the necessary paperwork to return to the States. New birth certificates were needed to apply for the children's passports. Notary signatures were necessary on every document. Government offices had already begun to close for the holidays. Desperation crept in.

I'd been in Ukraine for an entire month.

Saturday, December 30, I left all three kids with Jocelyn and Missy. Alexandra took me to the birth certificate office in Kasylviv. Though technically closed until January 9, a worker promised to meet Alex at 9:00 a.m. She agreed to process the new birth certificates for us. Alexandra and I waited in the frigid car for an hour and a half. I spent the time sprawled across the backseat begging God to send the woman our way.

A few minutes before 11:00 a.m. a woman arrived and unlocked the office. Alex motioned for me to join her inside the unlit building. Happy not to be left in the sardine can, I followed the two women through the glass entrance.

Inside, Alex and I stood in a waiting area lined with about a dozen chairs. The worker switched on the lights and seated herself at a clunky old computer. She pointed at the machine and spoke to Alexandra. The two women conversed for several minutes. I sensed a little tension and tried to figure out if they were arguing or making small talk. Either way, the matter appeared settled—the woman stood and surrendered her chair to Alex.

Grabbing a file from her tote bag, Alexandra said, "The worker does not know how to enter American names into the computer. She has agreed to let me do it. It will be faster for us."

As Alex clicked away on the old keyboard, I realized my prayers were being answered.

An hour later, she and I bounded out of the office jubilant with three new birth certificates. The official documents listed Wayne and Sandra Flach as the parents of Andrii Abraham Flach, Anna Esther Flach, and Jordan Charles Flach. We changed little Sergey's name to Jordan. Orphanage workers called him by the pet name "Serosha" instead of Sergey, and neither Ukrainian name fit his new life in America.

With the birth certificates in hand, Alexandra went in search of a notary to sign the documents. The only notary in Kasylviv refused to see us. We headed back in the direction of Kyiv and tried every notary office on the way. All were either closed or too busy to see us. Alex explained no one wanted the extra work since they were closing for the holidays. The refusal felt more personal to me—like nobody wanted to help the American lady. I cried the rest of the ride back to the apartment. When I got out of the car, I noticed Alex wipe a tear from her cheek.

Later that night, before turning out the light, I wrote Psalm 116:1-2 from the NLT in my journal: *"I love the Lord because He hears my voice and my prayer for mercy. Because He bends down to listen, I will pray as long as I have breath."* I fell asleep asking the Lord for mercy and the grace to carry on.

Jocelyn, Missy, and I spent New Year's Eve day wrangling our three Ukrainians. The morning began with the kids refusing to eat either cold cereal or oatmeal. Anna begged for candy or chips. They conceded to bananas and gobbled up all we had. I kept telling myself things will get easier once home on my own turf. For now, I just tried to survive and keep everyone alive.

After breakfast, all six of us bundled up for an adventure to the grocery store around the corner. I handed Andrii and Anna two Grivna, the equivalent of about fifty cents. They couldn't wait to buy potato chips and danced around us while we walked.

The store was alive with holiday hubbub like the mall back home. Busy shoppers, sparkling decorations, and Christmas music lifted my spirits. Missy and Jocelyn wrangled Andrii and Anna down the aisles while they bopped about in all the excitement. I pushed Jordan in an umbrella stroller we borrowed from Laura. The fun excursion gave me a glimpse of what life would be like once we got home—busy but good.

With grocery bags filled with bananas and chips, we exited the store. Outside, workers handed boxes of sparklers to the children. Free fireworks for kids seemed an unusual gift to us New Yorkers but Andrii and Anna were thrilled. I promised them we would light the sparklers outside when it got dark. They appeared satisfied with my idea and we headed down the street in the early afternoon sun.

Since the shopping trip was a success, we decided to stop at a playground near our building. The kids earned the reward and I desperately needed them to burn off some energy. Andrii and Anna darted toward the monkey bars excited to climb on something other than the walls. Jocelyn and Missy laughed and tried to keep up with them. Little Jordan giggled while I pushed him on a swing. The fresh, winter air invigorated my soul. I breathed deep, thankful to enjoy a second normal family activity with my new children. My serenity didn't last long, however.

Ten minutes later, Anna began rummaging through the shopping bags. She'd eaten all her chips and wanted to light sparklers. I tried to explain the need to wait until dark, but the language barrier made it difficult. Anna stormed off the playground and headed toward the apartment two blocks away.

Leaving Jordan dangling in his swing and trusting Jocelyn and Missy had witnessed Anna's escape. I chased her, praying the whole way. Andrii flew past me in determined pursuit of his sister. She made it into the building seconds ahead of us. I reached the elevator out of breath and too late—the door closed with Anna inside alone. I panicked. She did not know, which floor to get off. Andrii had already comprehended the situation and was running up the stairs adjacent to the elevator taking two steps at a time.

I knew he'd found her when the sound of children arguing in Ukrainian wafted down the elevator shaft. I didn't need a translator to figure out big brother was chastising little sister. Anna had made it up six flights to the top floor. Andrii brought her down to our second-floor apartment just as Jocelyn and Missy returned with Jordan.

Once we were all safely inside, I collapsed on the couch and called Laura. I told her what happened and asked her to explain to Anna that she must not run off again. Anna took the phone and listened while Laura spoke in Russian. She scowled but agreed to the new rule. She handed me the phone back and stomped off to the kitchen in search of more chips.

Later that evening we gathered outside and lit sparklers. The kids danced around, waved their magical wands, and laughed. Afterward, Jocelyn and Missy took Andrii and Anna to a New Year's Eve celebration at the YWAM base. I stayed back at the apartment with Jordan where I rang in the new year with an early bedtime for him and some quiet rest for me.

Ukraine rang in 2007 with more fireworks than the USA on Fourth of July. Celebratory flashes and booms, which began at 7:00 p.m. had lost their luster by the wee hours of the morning. I'd barely slept when Jordan awoke at 5:30 a.m. I took him potty and gave him some juice. He started to fall back to sleep when the grand finale lit up our bedroom at 6:00 a.m. We sat on my bed and watched the festivities just outside our window until the commotion finally died down.

Jordan drifted off to sleep again. Lying next to him, I watched his tiny tummy rise and fall. My heart swelled with love for this boy and his siblings. I didn't know what the future held, but it didn't matter—we were starting the new year as a family.

After an uneventful New Year's Day, I awoke on Tuesday morning, January 2, with a song running through my head based on 2 Corinthians 2:14: "Now thanks be to God who always leads us in triumph in Christ . . ." I pulled on my winter coat confident God was about to give me victory. Closing the apartment door quietly because Jocelyn, Missy and the kids were still sleeping, I left to complete some adoption business.

Outside, Alexandra and Stanislav were already waiting in the parking lot. We had a full agenda: head to the notary and then to passport offices in Bryankiv and Kasylviv. I opened the car door and slid into the backseat still praising God in my head—*Praise be to God who leads us in triumph . . .*

Alex turned around and smiled. In her heavy Ukrainian accent she said, "Good morning. Today in my country is holiday. Our government is closed. But we will try."

Holiday? Closed? We will *try*? The dreaded January shutdown was upon us. My heart sank like a deflated balloon. So much for victory and triumph. I wanted to scream. In the United States, we would never think about doing business at a government office on a holiday. But off to Bryankiv we went—to try.

We hadn't driven far when Alexandra spotted an open notary office and motioned for Stanislav to pull over. She invited me to go with her. Inside we stood by a long counter while Alex conversed with a woman seated at a desk on the other side. The woman looked over her glasses at Alex, then me, then back at Alex. She must have taken pity on this miserable-looking American woman because we left the office with notarized documents. But the small win failed to muster a glimmer of hope in me.

A half-hour later, we arrived in Bryankiv. Alexandra headed toward the passport office around the corner while I sat in the car under a weight of dejection. Unable to pray, I stared at the gray sky, which mirrored my mood.

Several minutes passed before I realized Alex had not returned to the car. A spark of hope flickered within me. If the office was closed, she would have come right back. Her absence meant something was happening. Faith kicked in and ignited my prayers. I begged God for victory.

After thirty minutes the car door opened. Cold January air spilled in with Alexandra. My eyes fixed on her. The news she carried held the power to lift my heart high or smash it to smithereens. Alex read the question on my face. With wide eyes she said, "The office was dark. The door was locked. But a woman let me in." Alex sounded as shocked as I felt. "The woman agreed to process our paperwork," she said, holding up Jordan's documents.

I sat in stunned silence—God had just worked a miracle.

Moments later, Stanislav whipped out of the parking lot and sped toward the passport office in Kasylviv. Andrii and Anna's documents still needed to be processed. I spent the hour bouncing back and forth between praising God and begging him for another miracle. We had just experienced God do the impossible in Bryankiv. Would He move mountains in Kasylviv too?

With no parking lot in sight, Stanislav found a spot on a snowy side street. Alexandra got out of the car and hustled to the passport office a block away. From the car I couldn't see the office, so I couldn't tell if the lights were on. Having no options, I huddled in the backseat and implored the Lord to move on our behalf again. Five minutes passed and Alex had not returned. Her delay fueled my prayers again. Every second she was gone meant good news. I prayed with everything in me, boldly beseeching God to perform another miracle.

After about forty minutes Alexandra returned to the car. She repeated almost the same scenario. The lights were off. The door locked. A woman inside the passport office let her in. Alex held up the completed documents.

I sat there speechless, wondering if I should repent for lack of faith or sing for joy? I did both.

With the taste of victory in our mouths and the necessary documents in hand, we headed to the central passport office in Kyiv where the actual passports are printed. During the ninety-minute ride, I pondered the miraculous events. Why would two women be at work in closed government offices in two different towns on the same day? Were they angels sent to help us? Maybe. But one thing I do know for sure—with God all things are possible.

The early-evening sky twinkled with stars when we arrived in Kyiv. I braced myself—this office would be closed too. Stanislav pulled into the parking lot. I looked out the window intrigued to see lights on inside the office building. Alexandra opened her door and motioned for me to join her.

We entered the unlocked doors just before 6:00 p.m. Inside, a handful of people milled around the dimly lit office. Alex left me in the waiting area while she spoke with a young woman working at a desk nearby. Tired of sitting in the car all day, I leaned against the wall and watched Alexandra approach the woman's desk and hand her a stack of documents. The two chatted and laughed like old friends. Twenty minutes later Alex smiled at me and headed toward the exit. I peeled myself off the wall and followed her out the door into the frigid night air.

"The girl is very nice," she said. "Our fathers have the same first name. Her middle name is Alexandra also. She said we can pick up the passports tomorrow by noon."

I had no idea how Alex discovered all those commonalities with the passport girl—and I didn't care. If we had the passports tomorrow, we could finish the process and be home in four days. Up until then, I had avoided torturing myself with thoughts of flying home. I didn't want to book our flights and have to cancel.

Now home felt within reach.

We still had to take all three kids for medical exams and have our documents stamped at the U.S. Embassy in Kyiv. But the passports meant we were almost home. On the way back to the apartment my heart sang, *"Praise be to God who leads us in His triumph . . . Praise be to God who's got the victory!"*

The next morning Andrii, Anna, Jordan, and I squeezed into the backseat of Stanislav's sardine can. Our smooshed but excited crew headed to the central passport office. True to the young woman's word, all three passports were ready. Our next stop—the American Medical Center.

The kids and I followed Alexandra into the clinic. About twenty patients lined the walls of a long hallway. Some sat and others leaned against the wall. On the way to our seats, I eyed the crowd and wondered how long we'd have to wait. Andrii and Anna took turns entertaining Jordan and agitating each other. The kids behaved well overall, but even I felt antsy. The physicals and a visit to the embassy were the only two steps between me and an airplane home.

After about thirty minutes a nurse called our number. The kids and I followed her into an exam room a few doors down from the waiting area. An English-speaking Ukrainian doctor performed a basic checkup on each child: listen to the heart and lungs, check reflexes, and open your mouth and say, "Ahh."

The doctor looked over all their medical records. He focused on Jordan's back—his spine twisted like a corkscrew because of severe scoliosis. The doctor recommended surgery, something we already anticipated. While examining Anna, he spent extra time listening to her heartbeat since her records indicated a heart murmur. The doctor didn't believe surgery would be necessary but suggested she see a cardiologist in the States. Andrii presented with no issues other than a lazy eye which could be corrected with eyeglasses. Overall the children were healthy, so the doctor signed our documents and approved their travel.

I released a long breath. Only one step left.

After the physicals, Alexandra directed Stanislav to the McDonald's drive-thru to celebrate. Andrii and Anna cheered. They loved McDonalds and begged to go every time we stepped outside the apartment. While they munched on French fries, I placed two phone calls I had been dying to make—the first to my travel agent and the second to Wayne. My anxious husband answered right away.

As soon as I heard his voice I choked up and started to cry. "I'm coming home," I blurted. "We fly out Saturday." After several seconds of silence Wayne could only manage to say, "Wow." I understood how he felt.

The next morning, Thursday, January 4, Alexandra and her brother picked the kids and me up at our apartment. We headed to the U.S. Embassy for the last step in the adoption process—the children's visas—necessary to enter the United States. Ten minutes later, Stanislav pulled the car up to the massive concrete fortress. The most amazing sight caught my eye—the American flag. I got out of the car with tears rolling down my checks. That flag was the first symbol of home I had seen in thirty-nine days.

Inside the embassy we navigated through the security line. At first, an officer stopped Alexandra from coming with me. I explained I needed her to help me with the three children while I completed the paperwork. The officer conceded. We hustled inside down a series of halls and through security doors. I took special note of every hint of America. Flags, a poster of an eagle, and signs in English all lifted my homesick spirit.

We reached the waiting room and discovered other American families on the same mission. A woman from Indianapolis waited with her four children. A couple from Kentucky adopting a girl. A family from Long Island adopting a boy. All waited their turn in line. We briefly exchanged stories. Most had been in Ukraine more than thirty days as well.

Alexandra led the children to a separate waiting area with toys. I took a seat and filled out several documents handed to me by a clerk. After a brief interview and more document signing, an official told me to come back at 4:00 p.m. to pick up the visas. I left disappointed but grateful he didn't say to come back tomorrow or next week.

Back at the apartment Jocelyn dished out soup and slices of bread and cheese. She kept us fed with home-cooked meals most days. The hot lunch filled my belly and warmed my heart with gratitude for my helpers. Jocelyn and Missy were in charge of the children while Alexandra dragged me around Ukraine on adoption business. I could not have managed without them.

After we ate, I organized our belongings. Packing made me giddy. Only two more days until we flew home.

Alex called and instructed me to be ready at 3:30 p.m. so Stanislav could take me back to the embassy to pick up the visas. Since the children didn't need to go with me this time, Jocelyn and Missy made plans to take them to visit the Stoltzfus's.

I breezed through the American Embassy with relative ease—in and out in under an hour. My heart soared when I left the building with three visas in my hands. Now we could go home. On the ride back I remembered the kids were all out. The apartment would be empty. I decided to celebrate the completed adoption with a long hot bath.

The phone was ringing when I walked through the apartment door. Without taking off my coat, I answered. Alexandra. "The orphanage director in Kasylviv called," she said. "The mayor heard we took the children before we were legally allowed to. He is threatening to have the director fired."

My weary brain tried to process this information.

"You don't have to do this," Alex continued. "But she is a nice director. Would you sign a document stating you took the children one day for passport pictures and one day for medical exams?"

Alexandra asked me to sign my name to a lie. I'm an honest person. Lying goes against my character. But something tugged on my heart. The director and all the staff had been hospitable to us. Andrii and Anna were possibly the first children adopted from the orphanage. I couldn't help but think we somehow paved the way for the next family. If the director got fired the staff might be reluctant to assist in future adoptions. I pictured the faces of the children left behind at the orphanage. Peace came over me. I knew what I needed to do.

Stanislav picked me up twenty minutes later. Instead of a hot bath I sank into a cold backseat in route to Kasylviv. I remembered how happy I was the day we picked up Andrii and Anna. I never thought I'd have to make this trip again. Now here I was speeding through the darkness on a strange mission. Fear of the unknown crept upon me. I drowned my thoughts in worship music from a compact disc player. My heart knew I made the right choice. But my mind tried to convince me otherwise.

We arrived in Kasylviv around 7:00 p.m. Instead of pulling into the orphanage parking lot, Stanislav drove into a vacant lot nearby. He turned the car off. We sat in the dark for a minute. I realized only Alex, Stan, and the Good Lord knew my whereabouts. Neither my family back home nor Jocelyn and Missy in Ukraine were aware of my mysterious excursion. If I disappeared, no one would know where to look for me.

Stan motioned for me to get out of the car. We both stood in eerie darkness. The only sound came from my heartbeat and the distant bark of a stray dog. I wondered if this was when the Russian Red Army would jump out of the bushes. They could drag me off to a forced labor camp in Siberia. No. I had a greater chance of being trafficked by the Russian mob.

While I considered my possible fate, the orphanage director appeared. She cried and babbled. I didn't understand her, and Stanislav couldn't translate. She handed me a pen and a clipboard with an official looking document attached. I had no idea what the letter said because it was printed in Ukrainian. I glanced at the bushes. No sign of a hostile takeover. After a quick, silent prayer, I held my breath and signed my name.

The director took the clipboard, smiled at my signature, and hugged me. Through tears she repeated, "Spa-see-buh," over and over, meaning *thank you*.

Stan motioned for me to get in the car. On the way back to Kyiv I wondered what had just happened. With worship music pulsing through my headphones, I praised God for protecting me from whatever danger lurked in the darkness of Kasylviv.

CHAPTER 9

Going Home

"This is the day the Lord has made;
I will rejoice and be glad in it!"

Psalm 118:24 NLT

Jocelyn, Missy, and I were going stir-crazy, and the kids were driving us there. Laura lent us a big bucket of tiny Legos for the older kids to play with. Little Jordan dumped the bucket every chance he got. After the fifth time of cleaning up a thousand plastic pieces, the blocks went back to the Stoltzfus apartment.

Andrii and Anna climbed the walls—literally. They figured out how to cling to the inside of the doorways with their bare feet and hands and crawl spider-like all the way to the ceiling. The kids needed to run and play outside. Six people crammed into a one-bedroom apartment was getting old. I hung on to my sanity by reminding myself only twenty-four more hours and we would be home.

We spent our last evening in Ukraine with the Stolzfus's. I used their computer to update my blog, send emails, and print our flight itinerary. I floated along on peace, joy, and gratefulness while finalizing travel details. Jocelyn and Missy entertained my kids along with the Stolzfus children. Little Jordan became overwhelmed by the excitement. I left early to put him to bed while Jocelyn, Missy, Andrii, and Anna stayed longer. Before I left, Laura and I hugged goodbye. Our parting bittersweet—I know I would not have sur-vived all those weeks in Ukraine without Laura and Joey. I'm forever grateful for their friendship and hospitality throughout the long ordeal.

Back at the apartment I put Jordan in the bathtub. He loved splashing in bubbles now. The first bath I tried to give him was like washing a screaming octopus. I had Alexandra ask him why he didn't like taking a bath. Jordan babbled something about a not-so-nice lady named Tonya. My second attempt included soothing warm water and an abundance of bubbles. He resisted at first, but I splashed the water and made a mountain of bubbly foam. Little Jordan stopped crying and started giggling. From that point on he loved taking a bath.

After bath time, I dressed Jordan in his red-footed pajamas. He roamed around the living room with a sippy cup of juice while I called Wayne with our flight itinerary. Jordan set his cup on a small, wooden table in the corner. Before I could stop him, he'd flipped the heavy table over and screamed. It had landed on his foot. I threw the phone down and ran to my boy, unzipped his pajamas and inspected his foot. Jordan's big but very tiny toe was decimated.

He screeched so loud I feared other tenants in the building would call the police. I'd probably watched too many movies and read too many books because images of the Red Army dragging me away flashed through my mind. Carrying Jordan's flailing body to the couch, I reached for the phone. Wayne was still on the line. I explained the commotion. We exchanged hurried goodbyes trusting we'd be together in twenty-four hours—as long as I wasn't languishing in a Ukrainian prison by then.

Jordan refused cuddles and all things mommies do to fix boo-boos. He did, however, drink the sweet children's liquid pain reliever

I offered him. I observed his purple, bloody toe from a distance while he sucked on his fingers and sobbed. After about thirty minutes, Jordan's sobs turned to fretful sighs and he gave in to sleep.

I dozed on and off until Jocelyn and Missy returned with the kids. When the girls tiptoed into my room, I pointed to Jordan's toe. They stared wide-eyed at the wound then retreated to go put Andrii and Anna to bed. Throughout the night my fitful sleep was interrupted each time Jordan stirred. I watched the clock, praying for morning to come.

January 6, 2007, after six weeks in Ukraine, I boarded a Delta flight with Missy, Jocelyn and my three children. We were going home. I buckled my seatbelt and settled in for the long, direct flight to JFK. Little Jordan curled up in the seat to my left. He wore only one shoe because of his toe. Andrii and Anna huddled together across the aisle on my right. They were excited to have TV screens mounted in the seats directly in front of them. Jocelyn and Missy sat somewhere behind us already engrossed in a movie. I gave liquid Benadryl to all three kids right before take-off—a tip I learned from another adoptive mom. Jordan was asleep before we left the ground. The older two conked out not long after. I dialed in on the screen in front of me and watched the little plane icon cross the Atlantic in slow motion.

Eight hours later, our uneventful flight landed at JFK in New York. We navigated through long customs lines with sleepy, shoeless Jordan in an umbrella stroller. Andrii and Anna followed along sluggishly. They perked up when I explained Papa would be there to meet us. While we waited, I noticed typical airport posters on the walls. I nudged Missy and pointed—the posters were in English. We laughed at the sudden surprise. After a month in Ukraine we had grown used to everything printed in a foreign language. We had even begun to decipher Russian words. Seeing English on a sign meant we were mere steps away from our waiting family.

I handed our sealed adoption documents over to a U.S. Immigration officer. He opened and processed them. His actions completed the final step in declaring Andrii, Anna, and Jordan official citizens of the United States. I released a long exhale. We'd made it through the legal procedure and were now free to find our anxious family.

Before I recognized anyone in the crowd, I heard my husband's voice call, "Andrii, it's Papa." From the corner of my eye, I saw my boy dart forward. I caught sight of Wayne on his knees just as Andrii dived into his daddy's arms.

In a sea of faces, I spied my mom, Sierra, and our friend Dennis Anderson. Dennis, familiar with the city, had driven the church van down from Albany to pick us up. Wayne Jr. and Curtis didn't come to the airport. They opted to attend youth group since there wouldn't be room for them in the van anyway.

My first welcome home hug came from my mom—an adoption skeptic. She had tears in her eyes from witnessing Wayne and Andrii's reunion. I introduced Mom to her three new grandchildren. She welcomed Andrii and Anna with bear hugs and a boisterous, "I'm your grandmother!" A bit shy and overwhelmed they both offered respectful hellos. Mom shook Jordan's tiny hand. Still in the umbrella stroller, he smiled with no idea what was happening around him. Wayne made his way over to me. I melted into his strong, comforting embrace.

We collected the luggage and settled our exhausted troupe into the van. After an hour, the conversation lulled. Most of our party snoozed. I leaned back in my seat and looked out at the darkness covering the Hudson Valley. While relieved the journey home had ended, I realized the adventure had only begun.

CHAPTER 10

A Brother Named Slava

"And God is able to bless you abundantly, so that in all things at all times, having all you need, you will abound in every good work."

2 CORINTHIANS 9:8 NIV

Those early weeks and months home with our kids are a blur in my memory. Countless doctor and dentist appointments filled my calendar. Andrii needed extensive dental work. His cavities required eleven dentist visits in twelve months. He got eyeglasses and tubes in his ears because of chronic ear infections. A cardiologist determined that Anna had a small hole in her heart called Mitral Valve Prolapse. Thankfully, she didn't need surgery. Little Jordan's crossed eyes did require surgery. His scoliosis turned out to be a complicated case requiring long-term treatment. Jordan would endure thoracic casting, growing rods, multiple surgeries and spinal fusion. We thanked God for a renowned spinal surgeon right in the Albany area.

Meal preparation became a popular production. Each afternoon, while I cooked dinner, Andrii and Anna hovered over me enthralled by the bubbling pots on the stove. They hadn't seen food prepared in the orphanage. The standard menu there was only a bowl of broth and piece of bread. My American kitchen offered variety and abundance. And they seemed to take much delight in watching me.

Intrigued by the sights and smells, Andrii nearly always would ask, "What is this?" How does one explain spaghetti and meatballs or cheesy chicken to a Ukrainian with limited English? It didn't matter. They devoured whatever I served. Fresh fruits and vegetables were a favorite of all three kids. Their deprived bodies needed to make up for years of poor nutrition.

Andrii, Anna, and Jordan clicked into our family with overall ease. We homeschooled our other kids for six years before adopting. Our plan to continue with the new children turned out to be the best choice for our family. Those early weeks home with all seven kids together helped us build relationships. Instead of everyone going separate ways each day, we were all home together. We got to know each other and bond as a family. Even in the midst of all the chaos, I treasured each busy day.

One afternoon as I cleaned up from lunch, our oldest son, Wayne Jr., approached me in the kitchen. "What would we do if there was ever another sibling in Ukraine?"

We had been home for six months. Wayne and I had not told any of our kids about little Slava still in the orphanage. Surprised by his question, but acting nonchalant, I answered with a question, "What makes you ask?"

"Well, we'd have to go get them. It wouldn't be fair to leave them there when we're all here."

My first-born just confirmed we had not ruined our family in the process of adopting. In the back of my mind, I had worried that we might do more harm than good. But even with three new siblings and a crazy household, Wayne Jr. was open to adding another brother or sister to the mix. I marveled at how the Lord might be opening the door to bring Slava. But I kept the secret.

By November 2007, Andrii had a good handle on English. During a three-hour drive home from a field trip to Plimoth Plantation, Sierra,

Andrii, Anna, and Jordan were settled into our SUV. From the backseat Andrii launched an unexpected question.

"Do you know I have a brother still in Ukraine?"

Wayne and I exchanged glances. We had no idea how Andrii knew about Slava. We still hadn't told anyone. And like with Jordan, Andrii and Anna had never met this younger sibling.

I inhaled. "Yes, we know."

From the backseat, Anna yelled, "Can we get him too?"

I laughed and exhaled. "His name is Slava. And yes, we will go get him too."

Just like that, the door to Slava flew open. Well sort of. Wayne and I let Andrii and Anna share this news with the rest of the family. Our biological kids and even my parents agreed—we must bring Slava home.

By now it should be no surprise—bringing an orphan out of darkness and into light will trigger enemy opposition. Getting Slava home would not be easy. In January 2008 we contacted Andrew Parker, our lead facilitator in Ukraine and Alexandra's boss. We needed to find out if Slava was available for adoption yet.

Alexandra visited the orphanage and the courthouse in Bryankiv. Her investigation revealed that Slava, now two years old, still lived in the orphanage but his name was not in the database of adoptable orphans. At the courthouse, Alex discovered he was not available for adoption because the rights of his biological parents had not been terminated.

Wayne and I stood firm. We wanted our son. To grease the wheels of the slow-moving system, we hired Andrew and his team again. Alexandra made regular trips to the orphanage to remind the director and staff that Slava had a family coming for him.

She also visited the courthouse. Slava's file was just one in a stack collecting dust. With no one advocating for him, his file would stay at the bottom of the pile. He would remain an orphan. Before Slava could become our son, a court hearing to terminate parental rights needed to occur. Alex pushed for this hearing, and in the process learned the children's biological mother had passed away.

This news broke my heart. The kid's birth mother was often on my mind and in my prayers. I felt sure she somehow knew her children had been adopted and moved far away to the United States. I had no proof of this. How could she have known? My heart ached for this woman whose tremendous loss was my treasured gain.

Court documents revealed the young woman died three months after we brought the kids home—at age twenty-seven. In Ukraine, the cause of death is not listed on death certificates, so we didn't know how she died. Either way, her passing further complicated the process for us to adopt Slava.

Alexandra worked on our behalf to maintain favor with the orphanage director in Bryankiv. At home, I rallied our church and collected children's coats, hats, and shoes. We shipped them to Ukraine and Alex delivered the gifts to the orphanage. She also brought fresh fruit and cookies for all the children with money we sent. The director and staff appreciated the donations, and we were happy to do something positive for our little boy and the other orphans.

After delivering the clothing, Alexandra emailed me a picture of Slava dressed in a new coat. He smiled at the camera with a mouthful of banana. I clung to the picture and prayed for our little boy who grew in our hearts and became part of our family before he ever set foot on American soil. I hated how slow the adoption wheels turned in Ukraine. While I waited to travel the first time, adoption consumed me. This time around, however, my large family kept me too busy to dwell on it every minute of the day. Most of the time anyway.

In April 2008, our daughter Missy traveled back to Ukraine on another short-term mission with our church. Much like our trip in 2004, the team volunteered at the YWAM base in Kyiv. Hoping Alexandra could arrange a visit for Missy to meet Slava, I sent along a small photo album containing pictures of our happy family, including Andrii, Anna, and Jordan. My plan was for Missy to show her little brother the pictures and give the orphanage director the album to keep.

I plopped down at my computer with giddiness and emailed Alex about Missy's arrival in Kyiv. Her response shouldn't have surprised me, but I got caught up imagining Missy and Slava meeting for the first time. Alexandra reported that seeing Slava wouldn't be possible . . . but she would try. My disappointment was only temporary. I knew what God could do when Alex said she would try. I prayed God would make a way where there seemed to be no way. After all, nothing is impossible for Him—we had three children to prove it.

Two days later, Alex sent word that she had made arrangements for a visit. She would pick Missy up the following day and take her to Bryankiv. The next day, I checked my email every thirty minutes. In the evening I finally received an email from Missy. Alexandra cancelled the visit. She had no idea why. I chided myself for getting my hopes up again. Nothing in Ukraine ever happens as expected.

Early the next afternoon, a surprise email arrived from Missy. I couldn't open it fast enough. When I did, it revealed a picture of Missy holding Slava on her hip. They were standing in the familiar orphanage playroom. Missy explained that an early-morning phone call from Alex roused her from sleep. Minutes later she was in the backseat of a car on the way to Bryankiv. Missy spent an hour with her little brother. Alex took the picture of them together—a snapshot I still treasure.

In early fall 2009, Andrew reported that legal proceedings were completed. Four-year-old Slava had been declared a legal orphan. But, in true Ukrainian adoption style, this highlight came with a low blow.

Andrew explained that in Ukraine, the first calendar year a child was a legal orphan, they are not eligible for international adoption. We hadn't heard of this law before. Regardless, for the next 365 days, Slava could only be adopted domestically. Most Ukrainian families were too poor to adopt, but there were no guarantees a family wouldn't swoop in and take him. The news felt like a sick joke. Our little boy would remain in the orphanage for another year before we were permitted to adopt him.

Wayne and I had no legal rights to Slava, but we would fight to bring him home. We had adopted his biological siblings, but the Ukrainian government didn't seem to care. Our only course of action—prayer and persuasion. We prayed Ukraine would waive the law that kept us from our son.

With due diligence, I submitted our post-adoption reports to the Ukrainian Embassy in New York City. These annual reports are a required part of the post-adoption process until the children are eighteen. It's a way for Ukraine to confirm the legitimacy of adoption and safety of the children. Reports include medical, dental, educational, and well-being updates accompanied by pictures. I made sure to include a plea for Slava along with the paperwork.

We tried to expedite the process by sending letters to the State Department for Adoption in Kyiv. Andrii and Anna each wrote a letter pleading for their little brother. We included a photograph of Andrii, Anna, and Jordan holding a picture of Slava. I believed if anything could melt a cold heart this photo was it. Who would deny uniting these precious children?

Nothing worked. We waited the year out in the U.S., while our little boy remained in Ukraine without a family.

We are grateful for Andrew Parker and his capable facilitation team. They submitted our dossier to the SDA in September 2010—strategically timed so we would be approved for travel the same month Slava would be available for international adoption.

After three years of waiting, the time to bring Slava home had come. Our little boy turned five years old on October 16, 2010. We arrived in Ukraine a week later, my heart filled with awe at God's timing.

Slava would receive the best birthday present ever—a family.

CHAPTER 11

Back to Ukraine

"You can ask for anything in my name, and I will do it,
so the Son can bring glory to the Father."

JOHN 14:13 NLT

Wayne and I, along with seven-year-old Jordan, arrived in Kyiv, Ukraine on Saturday, October 23, 2010. We brought Jordan along for two reasons. First, because he's our youngest, we didn't think he would do well without us for several weeks. Second, we believed his presence would make the transition less scary for Slava. For our first adoption, Andrii, Anna, and Jordan had each other for the journey home. Slava would be alone. I hoped the two brothers would bond and become best buddies. Little did I know the impact five years in an orphanage would have on our newest son.

The thrill of adventure pulsed through me when we landed in Ukraine. The desperation I experienced three years earlier had worn off—like a mother forgets pains of childbirth as she hopes for another baby. I was ready to fight the good fight and bring our boy home.

We celebrated a mini-family reunion at the airport. Our precious Alexandra and her driver-brother, Stanislav, welcomed us with hugs. They picked us up in their new, small SUV. No more tiny tin can. Wayne, Jordan, and I loaded into the spacious backseat excited to embark on the escapade ahead.

After a stop at a nearby grocery store, the duo delivered us to our accommodations near Kyiv's popular Independence Square. Our apartment was located up the street from another bustling McDonald's. Wayne and Jordan cheered when we drove by the restaurant. The modern flat satisfied my taste for home. It was clean, had a washing machine, and an internet connection.

Internet in the apartment made communicating with the kids back home easier. We'd left Anna, now eleven, Andrii thirteen, and Sierra fourteen in the capable hands of Curtis, now eighteen, and Melissa, twenty. My parents agreed to check on them each day as would Wayne Jr. and his wife, Kerri, who married four months earlier and lived nearby.

Exhausted but thrilled to be back in Ukraine, Wayne, Jordan, and I settled into our new abode. We had two days to rest up for our official appointment at the SDA. While I unpacked our suitcases and put away the groceries, my hands trembled. I could not stop thinking about our little Slava. We were just forty-eight hours away from meeting him.

I had romantic notions of Slava's homecoming. Andrii, Anna, and Jordan adjusted with virtual ease into our family. So well, in fact, we thought of ourselves as adoptive parenting pros. Last time, we adopted three kids at once. How hard could it be to bring home one little five-year-old? But we were about to learn how much havoc one little five-year-old can wreak on an ill-prepared family.

The moment I anticipated for so long, finally arrived—appointment day. On Monday, October 25, 2010, Alexandra escorted us into the same building we'd entered for our first adoption in 2006. During that appointment was when we first saw those sad pictures of Andrii, Anna, and Jordan. Now we were here for

Slava. I shook my head. I experienced deja vu and dreams-come-true at the same time.

Alex directed us to a hallway lined with chairs. We sat with other couples and waited our turn. No one talked. Each family, when their number was called, was about to make a life-changing decision. We kept Jordan, the only one in the room without a care in the world, occupied with candy and a round of eye-spy.

Twenty minutes later, Alexandra alerted us that our turn had come. Years earlier, we went into the appointment alone. Now the rules had changed, and we entered the meeting with Alex by our side.

A beautiful young woman with long brown hair motioned toward a row of chairs in the corner of the office. We took our seats—Wayne on my right with Jordan on his lap and Alex on my left. The woman seated herself next to Alex. She opened the file on her lap and held up a picture of Slava. Alexandra translated for us.

"Do you want to adopt this boy?"

Wayne and I answered in unison. "Yes!"

Her next question baffled me.

"Why do you want to adopt this boy?"

Seriously? But realizing there must be a protocol to follow, I played along. "We adopted this child's older siblings three years ago," I said. "We already consider him our son."

I watched the woman while Alex translated but couldn't tell what she was thinking. Wayne handed her a small photo book he'd retrieved from his backpack. She glanced at the pictures while I carefully pointed out Andrii, Anna, and Jordan—each happy and surrounded by family. Alexandra stopped translating for a moment. The woman said something to her. With a hint of irritation Alex translated my photo descriptions.

The two women exchanged a few more words in Russian then stood. That was it. The entire appointment lasted fifteen minutes. As we grabbed our coats, Jordan announced, "Now we can go see Slava!" We hushed him and headed to the car.

Alex had gotten permission from the orphanage director for us to meet Slava that day. Typically, a family must wait for a referral document to be processed which takes a day or two. We didn't have to wait because the director liked us—maybe because we'd adopted Jordan from there three years earlier or because of all those gifts we'd sent. Whatever the reason, we were only an hour from seeing our boy.

On our way to Bryankiv, Alexandra explained her frustration during the appointment. "The woman at the SDA is my friend. She knows English."

I rolled my eyes. SDA officials actually understand every word spoken by prospective adoptive parents. Even words couples whisper to each other as they navigate through pictures of orphans while making life-changing decisions. It didn't seem fair. But we must have passed the test.

My heart beat faster when we approached the familiar cement-block building. I wondered what Jordan was thinking. Would he think we were giving him back? What if he had bad memories? Jordan had been three years old when we adopted him. He never talked about the orphanage. We weren't sure how this visit would affect him, but we were about to find out.

My concerns evaporated with the slam of a car door. Jordan jumped out of the parked vehicle and darted toward the building. We ran to keep up with him.

Inside the unheated lobby, Jordan's arrival drew immediate attention. Five women surrounded our boy. His previous caregivers were excited to see their "Serosha" again. The poor kid was surrounded by a gaggle of grandmothers trying to kiss his face and pinch his cheeks. The women looked him over and nodded their approval. They tried speaking to him, but he no longer understood Ukrainian. Jordan started to back away. Alex swooped in and rescued him.

She led us upstairs to the familiar playroom, the same place we first visited Jordan. The same ball pit, primary-colored mats, and riding toys filled the space. Too antsy to sit, I paced. Any minute a caregiver would arrive with Slava. I anticipated this moment since the day I shook his tiny hand four years earlier. I stared at the door willing it open. And it did.

With a sudden burst, the door flew open and Slava bounded into the room. The staff had told him his mama, papa and brother were coming for him. A worker shared that he was excited to see us. He'd been pestering them for days about our arrival. He was excited all right.

Slava bounced about like the little silver ball in a pinball game. We coaxed him to sit with us by offering half a banana. He shoved the whole thing into his mouth and begged for more. He gobbled up two whole bananas and two cookies in less than a minute. When I ran out of food, he ditched me and darted over to the riding toys.

Wayne tried to entice him with other toys, but Slava preferred throwing over playing. Jordan stood off to the side avoiding his little brother's path. He had a shell-shocked expression on his face. We were all relieved when, twenty minutes later, Slava's caregiver came back and took him to lunch.

The visit felt more like an ordeal than a family reunion. While we waited for Alexandra to come back for us, Wayne said, "What are we going to do when they tell us we can take him?"

I confessed the same apprehension and wondered how we would get this wild bundle of energy home on an airplane.

Court documents revealed Slava had been born to an alcoholic mother and abandoned at birth. Exposure to alcohol in the womb and five years in an institution where he suffered further neglect, malnourishment, and lack of nurture describe his crucial developmental years. After that first visit, I realized completing this adoption was only our first hurdle. We were about to embark on a new road—parenting a child with special needs.

But I didn't care what lay ahead. Slava was already our son in my heart and soon we would have the documentation to prove it. I was determined to bring him home and braced myself for the challenge.

In the car on the way back to Kyiv, Alexandra updated us on the adoption climate in Ukraine. The government was now giving money to families to help prevent children from entering the orphanage system. The program sounded similar to the welfare system in the United States. She also said more Ukrainian families were adopting. Young, healthy children and babies were being adopted not long after they arrive at an orphanage. These two developments meant there were less children in orphanages. The news sounded good until Alex's tone turned ominous.

"We had to make war every day and every week for Slava."

Startled, I leaned closer to catch every word.

"Because he is healthy other families want to adopt him. I had to visit the orphanage every week to remind them you were coming. You must visit Slava every day. People are watching. You have to prove you want this child."

During the four years we waited to get Slava, I never imagined a Ukrainian family snatching him up. Daily trips to Bryankiv would be exhausting and visits with our boy challenging. But it didn't matter. God chose Slava to be our son. We would do whatever we needed to take him home.

Each morning, before leaving the apartment, I spent time reading my Bible and praying. Chapters 5 and 6 in the Gospel of John resonated with me. Jesus healed people and fed the multitudes. These verses taught me that Jesus, in the supernatural, can do what we cannot do in the natural. In Ukraine, Wayne and I were powerless. By ourselves we could do nothing. But with God, all things are possible. I prayed for God to move in the supernatural on our behalf.

Slava's process did not involve direct opposition from government officials like our first adoption. We did, however, encounter some paperwork snags along the way. Slava's birth mom's death certificate had her maiden name on it. All the other documents, such as Slava's birth certificate, had her married name on them. I didn't allow this detail to drag me down. I trusted God and Alexandra to work it all out.

Adoptions, like mission trips, are times of great personal growth. For this trip to Ukraine I brought along the book *Tales of Brokenness* by Don Nori in which he writes, "He fitted you to Himself like a glove into which He slips His hand to accomplish His purposes. So, by yourself you cannot accomplish what God created you to do. You need His Spirit to fulfill your destiny." The message that *I am the glove; God is the hand* motivated me for my daily mission.

Wednesday, November 3, 2010, my morning devotion included reading John 14:13-14 NLT where Jesus said, "You can ask for anything in my name and I will do it, because the work of the Son brings glory to the Father. Yes, ask anything in my name, and I will do it!"

We had been waiting and praying for our Interpol clearances to arrive in Kyiv and for a court date with the judge. Like before, the ten-day wait doesn't begin until you meet with the judge. The Interpol clearances were a new piece to the adoption process. State and federal background checks were always part of the procedure. Now international clearances had to be obtained. We could not get a court date without Interpol clearance. Yet another step that complicated the process and lengthened the wait. A familiar desperation crept over me.

I read John 14:13-14 to Wayne. Together we prayed and reminded God that He said we could ask anything in the name of Jesus. We specifically asked Him for our clearances to arrive and for an immediate court date—in Jesus' name.

An hour after we prayed Alexandra called to say our clearances were in. Instead of waiting for them to be delivered, she picked them up. Soaring with hope, I asked how long before we could expect a court date? "I am good friends with this judge. I just met with her. We have a court day for tomorrow."

Exhilaration overcame my desperation. I hung up the phone and shared the news with Wayne. We hugged, lifted our hands in praise, and thanked God. That night I laid awake pondering how we really can ask for anything in Jesus' name and He will do it.

CHAPTER 12

Slava Joseph Flach

"But if you remain in me and my words remain in you,
You may ask anything you want, and it will be granted!"

JOHN 15:7 NLT

T hursday, November 4, 2010, unfolded a different court
experience from our adoption four years earlier. My first clue
to the odd proceedings came when we pulled up to the courthouse.
The cement block building was painted Barney purple.

Because the judge agreed to see us during her lunch break, we
met in her cramped office. No intimidating courtroom or cage this
time. Wayne and I stood by the judge's desk in the only empty space
not occupied by files and ledgers. According to Alexandra, the judge
"made us many favors" because she liked Alex. Grateful for their
friendship, the unusual lack of formality helped ease my nerves.

The judge asked us familiar questions. "Why do you want to
adopt this child? What is your name and address? Where does
Wayne work? What is your income? Do you have enough money?
Do you have health insurance? What do you want to change the
child's name to?"

We answered the questions and addressed the name change. The
judge whipped out a gavel and slammed it on her desk. Her seal-of-
approval proclaimed Slava a Flach and triggered the ten-day wait.

My celebratory mood ended when we got in the car and
Alexandra delivered some disappointing news. The process had

changed a bit since our last adoption. We'd still have to apply for a new birth certificate but now there was an identification number, similar to a Social Security number, to deal with. After that, we could apply for Slava's passport. But there was a new process for that too—and it took five days.

Like before, we needed the new birth certificate and passport before we could take Slava for a physical at the American Medical Clinic. When all those steps were completed, we could finish at the U.S. Embassy and fly home. Alex listed off the to-do items and dread threatened to steal my joy. I fought off the feeling of desperation by reminding myself that with God all things were possible.

Back at the apartment I pulled out my calendar. Although it was early November, a nagging feeling crept up my neck. Between the ten-day wait and the rest of the process we could end up spending Thanksgiving in Ukraine. I had missed Christmas and New Year's for our first adoption in 2006. I dreaded the thought of losing another holiday with my family back home.

Every day we connected with our kids in the U.S. through Skype and Facebook. Seeing their faces on the screen and hearing their voices helped ease my mind. My parents and the older kids were managing with Sierra, Andrii, and Anna. Everyone seemed fine, but I desperately wanted to be home by Thanksgiving. I prayed God would move on our behalf and expedite the process.

Our ten-day wait began the first day after court. That morning my Bible reading was from John 15. These are some of my favorite portions of Scripture:

> *"But if you remain in me and my words remain in you, you may ask for anything you want, and it will be granted! When you produce much fruit, you are my true disciples. This brings great glory to my Father."*

JOHN 15:7-8 NLT

"You didn't choose me. I chose you. I appointed you to go and produce lasting fruit, so that the Father will give you whatever you ask for using my name. This is my command: Love each other."

Jᴏʜɴ 15:16-17 NLT

I had grown in my faith and understood God doesn't call the equipped, but He equips the called. God called us to adopt again. Though we didn't feel qualified, He chose us to parent these children. The days, weeks, months, and years ahead might be challenging, but He would provide and equip us for the challenge. We just needed to remain in Him.

Late that afternoon, Stanislav took us to Bryankiv for a visit with Slava. Usually the staff directed us outside to the orphanage playground. The large yard was equipped with old swings, rusty slides painted in bright colors, and plastic houses. We tried to keep up with Slava as he darted about, but he wore us out.

Because the evening approached, our visit was held inside. A caregiver led us to a little room containing only a couch, two chairs, and a shelf with a few broken toys on it. The small area meant no chasing. I sighed, grateful for the reprieve.

Wayne and I approached these visits with a sense of joy and dread. We loved Slava and wanted to bring him home. At the same time, we feared what bringing him home would be like. The little boy's behavior was out of control. At the orphanage, we felt powerless. We feared if we tried to discipline him, a caregiver might take him away. I kept thinking, *When we get him home on our turf, things will improve.* But deep down inside, I knew we were in over our heads.

To maintain our sanity and manage Slava's behavior, we learned to bring toys with us. Bubbles were his favorite. Slava permitted Wayne to hold him so he could reach and pop the bubbles. Wayne used the opportunity to pray for our son. He asked God to give Slava peace instead of fear and to calm him and help him trust us. We didn't see any immediate changes but believed God would work in his heart.

That day, just before 6:00 p.m., Slava tried to tell us something. He went to the door, pointed up at the clock, and jabbered at us. He repeated this performance three or four times. On other visits he'd attempted to escape, but this time seemed different. He was very insistent. Without a translator we had no idea what he was trying to tell us. To find help, I opened the door and peeked into the hallway to see if any orphanage staff were around. Before I could catch him, Slava bolted down the hall, across the empty lobby, and up two flights of bright green and purple painted stairs. I panicked and ran after him.

Parents weren't permitted in other parts of the orphanage. While I pursued Slava, I worried a team of babushkas might tackle me to the ground. I almost caught him at the top of the rainbow stairs, but he flew down another hallway. I lost sight of him when he darted into a room. In my socks, I slid to a stop at the doorway. I peeked inside and saw about ten children sitting in a circle on little potty chairs. Slava knew it was potty time. Several women buzzed around tending to the children. They laughed at this exasperated mama. Embarrassed but relieved they didn't tackle me, I waved *paka* to my little boy happily seated on his potty.

CHAPTER 13

Iron Mama and Wild Child

"But those who hope in the LORD will renew their strength.
They will soar on wings like eagles; they will run and not grow
weary, they will walk and not be faint."

ISAIAH 40:31 NIV

F ive days into the ten-day wait, Stanislav took Jordan, Wayne, and me to the Museum of The History of Ukraine in World War II. We got to visit the Motherland Monument, which reminded us a bit of the Statue of Liberty. The immense silver gleaming statue could be seen from a distance on our many travels around Kyiv. We nicknamed her "Iron Mama." The tourist activity gave us a much-needed break from the grueling adoption process.

We appreciated the opportunity to learn some Ukrainian history. My stomach lurched as I viewed the gut-wrenching display of hundreds of old shoes taken from Ukrainian citizens herded off to concentration camps. Jordan, too young to understand the sobering scenes, wandered around the museum with us. He loved sitting in the military helicopter and airplane on display outside.

After the museum tour we headed to Bryankiv. This visit with Slava turned out to be the most draining yet. The orphanage staff bundled him in winter layers and sent us outside. I groaned. Playground time should be fun, but not with our wild child.

It took three of us to manage Slava on the slide. Wayne shadowed him as he bobbed and dipped up the ladder. I stood guard on the side since he had a habit of flinging himself down the slide. Stanislav caught him at the bottom to make sure he didn't escape. And Jordan hid behind me careful to stay out of his brother's path. This scenario played out a dozen exhausting times before Slava dashed off to the next piece of equipment.

Inside visits were just as stressful. Even though Slava was five, he did not understand how to play with toys. He either threw them or banged on them hammer-style with other toys until they broke. One time he pounded the wall with a toy truck and an orphanage worker came in and scolded us for making noise. Slava didn't seem phased.

That day, after an exhausting hour on the playground, we took him inside. I shrugged off my coat and collapsed on the couch. At least he would be contained in the little visitation room. My relief didn't last long. Slava ransacked my backpack looking for food and juice boxes. I intercepted the bag and handed out snacks to him and Jordan.

Sitting on the floor, I stacked wooden blocks in an attempt to engage both boys. Jordan joined me constructing his own tower. Slava came up from behind and pulled my hair. Stunned, I grabbed my hair and shouted, "No. Nee-yet." Slava laughed. Tears filled my eyes. Defeated by his antics and disappointed in my own reaction, I just wanted to go home.

Minutes later an orphanage worker came for Slava. The visit ended. Relief washed over me. Waving hasty goodbyes, we grabbed our coats. While tugging on my zipper, I realized that before long, Slava would be leaving with us. There would be no escape then.

Back in our apartment that night, Wayne and I wondered how we would survive parenting Slava. Initially, I cajoled myself by thinking things would improve when we got him home and I was more in control. I would set boundaries, dole out discipline, and teach this kid a thing or two. Now we faced a grim reality—Slava's behavior revealed signs of Fetal Alcohol Spectrum Disorder (FASD).

FASDs are a wide range of permanent effects that can occur in an individual whose mother consumed alcohol during pregnancy. These effects may include physical, mental, behavioral, and/or learning disabilities, which can have lifelong implications. I understood a little bit about the symptoms from researching FASD prior to our 2006 adoption. While common in orphans from Eastern Europe and children in the U. S. foster care system, neither Andrii, Anna, nor Jordan exhibited the symptoms we saw in Slava. Wayne and I were not equipped to parent a child with an FASD.

With three days left of our ten-day wait, Wayne got a call from his office back home. Good news—his industrial construction company secured a big job at a local plastics plant. Not good news—they wanted him home right away to manage it. I burst into tears.

Our original plan was for Wayne to return home after the court hearing just as he had done during our 2006 adoption. He could have left seven days ago. However, we both knew I couldn't handle Slava and Jordan myself. And Jordan insisted, if daddy was going home, so was he.

Wayne believed he should stay in Ukraine with me. But I knew he also felt the demands of his job. God knew our kids at home needed us. He knew Wayne had to get back to work. He knew Jordan wanted to go home. and Slava needed a family.

Our faith was being tested. We had to trust God and remember His faithfulness. Wayne and I held hands and prayed together. We asked for wisdom on whether Wayne should stay with me or return home. We also prayed for peace with our decision.

The next morning, I woke up thinking about Jesus feeding the crowd of 5,000 with five loaves of bread and two fish. The miracle recorded in Mark 6:30-41 occurs again two chapters later in Mark 8:1-16. Jesus and his disciples faced another large crowd—this time 4,000 hungry souls. When Jesus instructed his disciples to feed the people, they seemed to suffer memory loss. In Mark 8:4 AMP they asked, "Where will anyone be able to find enough bread here in this isolated place to feed these people?" I used to think I would have remembered the 5,000. I would have said, "Jesus, do that bread and fish thing again!"

I wondered why they failed to remember the first miracle. Then I realized my arrogance—we were doing the same thing. The Lord moved in amazing ways at the beginning of this adoption process. He moved mountains four years earlier for our first adoption as well. Now, during the ten-day wait, we were discouraged and doubtful about the obstacles ahead. We had forgotten the miracles of the past because we focused only on our present circumstances.

I shared the Scriptures with Wayne and explained what I believed the Lord was showing me. Together we repented for lack of faith. We thanked God for His faithfulness and prayed for His continued guidance. I even mustered up enough boldness to ask Him to bring us home by Thanksgiving.

By the next morning, Wayne had a sense that God wanted him to remain in Ukraine. If all went well, we could be home in two weeks anyway. He chose to stay with me and manage the job by phone and email. We both experienced peace with his decision.

The last day of our ten-day wait was Sunday, November 14. However, when Alexandra went to pick up our Court Decree on Monday the main judge said we could not have it until the next day. He cited some law which states if the tenth day is a Sunday, then one more day is added. Now Monday would be our tenth day, so the decree could not be picked up until Tuesday. Annoyed by this slight setback we headed to the orphanage for a visit.

In the visitation room, I sat on the floor and tried to engage Slava in play. He pulled my hair again and laughed at my stern, "No, nee-yet." I picked him up and set him on my lap for a time-out, which lasted only five seconds. Slava wiggled off and resumed ransacking the room. He threw toys and broke a plastic hammer we had brought for him.

Orphanage visits were frustrating because we were more visitors than parents. We had no authority. I kept telling myself things would improve once we got Slava home. We would be in charge. Things would be different.

I hoped.

CHAPTER 14

Surviving Slava

*"... to comfort all who mourn, and provide for those who grieve
in Zion—To bestow on them a crown of beauty instead of ashes,
the oil of joy instead of mourning, and a garment of praise instead
of a spirit of despair. They will be called oaks of righteousness, a
planting of the LORD for the display of his splendor."*

ISAIAH 61:3 NIV

O n Tuesday, November 16, 2010, Stanislav and Alexandra
picked us up in their small SUV. With Jordan, Wayne and
I packed in the backseat, we headed for Bryankiv to get the court
decree. Then off to birth certificate offices in Kasylviv and Bryankiv.
Paperwork needed to be processed in both villages because Slava was
born in one and lived in the other.

We spent an entire day in the backseat of a car. We passed the
time playing eye-spy and thumb wars with Jordan. At least we had
Slava's new birth certificate in hand. I allowed myself to exhale a
satisfying sigh. Movement forward in the process meant we were
closer to going home.

While the car whizzed back toward Kyiv, Alexandra rifled
through the documents in her brief case and checked her watch.
"We must go to the registration office. Slava's name must be changed
on his registration card."

I stifled a groan, looked at Wayne, and rolled my eyes. There
always seemed to be a new step in the process.

Late that afternoon, Stan dropped Alex off at the registration office. We stayed in the car and occupied Jordan with yet another round of eye-spy. Thirty minutes later Alexandra returned. She explained the new electronic system would not compute Slava's new name. Something about the *Joseph Flach* being a foreign language. They told her it could take up to five days to fix.

Five days? I shook my head. Why is it always five days? Why couldn't it be five minutes? I wanted to scream. Instead, I prayed.

Stanislav dropped us off at our apartment and Alexandra went to the main tax office in Kyiv to see if something could be done about the registration card. Wayne and I spent some time together in prayer about this new roadblock. Peace settled over us, so we stepped out in faith and scheduled our return flight home for November 25. We also booked a flight for our daughter Melissa, who at twenty, still loved Ukraine and its people. Missy was more than happy to fly over to help us home with the boys.

Minutes after booking the flights, my cell phone rang. Alex reported she'd already straightened out the registration number problem. I hung up in awe of how God had melted another obstacle like wax on our behalf.

The next day dawned sunny and warm—unusual for mid-November in Ukraine. Wayne and I welcomed the warmth. Our first adoption occurred in December 2006. Back then we spent most of our time freezing in the backseat of a cold car. Now the temperature neared sixty degrees Fahrenheit. We headed out to apply for Slava's passport and left our winter coats behind.

Before going to the central passport office in Kyiv, Alexandra needed to process paperwork at the passport office in Bryankiv. Wayne, Jordan, and I waited in the car for an hour. Several rounds of eye-spy later, she returned with bad news.

"The main man whose signature we need only works on Tuesday," she said.

Are you kidding me? Only one day a week and it was yesterday? I resisted an eyeroll and slumped back into my seat.

Before I had a chance to say anything, Alex added, "His secretary said he might make a special trip into the office later today." She looked at Wayne and then at me. "We can wait. It's up to you."

We exchanged glances and nodded. What other choice did we have?

To pass the time, Alexandra and Stanislav took us to a local cafe. After lunch, seven-year-old Jordan and I needed to use the bathroom. The restaurant was upscale, so I expected modern amenities. The clean lavatory sparkled with shiny, ivory-colored tile—right up to the porcelain sink-like hole in the floor. Jordan had no trouble doing his business. But I needed assistance. My leg muscles were not used to squatting. Jordan held onto my hands so I didn't fall in. He snickered at my balancing act. By the time I finished, we could not stop giggling. Jordan hoisted me up. Our laughter echoed off the tile walls. The ridiculous incident provided some comic relief from the stressful day.

Three hours later we drove back to the passport office in Bryankiv. Alex got the main man's signature. We left the village with completed documents but too late to go to the passport office in Kyiv.

Thursday morning Alexandra called. I braced myself. Weary from twenty-five days of one step forward and five steps back. She started with good news—I almost forgot what that felt like. Alex said, "The central passport office in Kyiv has all the necessary documents to make Slava's passport." She paused. "But it takes five to seven days to process a passport now."

Of course it does.

"The girl in the passport office is very nice. Maybe she will do it faster."

Of course she is.

I hung up the phone. The familiar roller coaster feeling threatened my stomach. After relaying Alexandra's news to Wayne, we did the math. There were two business days left in the week. And only eight days until our flight home. I dreaded the thought of rescheduling. That old desperate feeling rolled in like fog.

Before bed, Wayne and I lifted up another plea to the Lord. Our specific prayer request: get Slava's passport in time to make our November 25 flight home.

I couldn't sleep. My mind refused to shut off. To distract my frazzled brain, I listened to worship music on my iPod. In the middle of one song the device inexplicitly switched to another—*The Spirit of the Sovereign Lord is Upon Me* from the Brownsville Revival. God got my attention. The fog cleared. I knew He spoke to me through this song based on Isaiah 61:

> *"The Spirit of the Sovereign LORD is upon me, because the LORD has anointed me to proclaim good news to the poor. He has sent me to bind up the brokenhearted, to proclaim freedom for the captives and release from darkness for the prisoners, to proclaim the year of the LORD's favor and the day of vengeance of our God, to comfort all who mourn, and provide for those who grieve in Zion—to bestow on them a crown of beauty instead of ashes, the oil of joy instead of mourning, and a garment of praise instead of a spirit of despair. They will be called oaks of righteousness, a planting of the LORD for the display of his splendor. They will rebuild the ancient ruins and restore the places long devastated; they will renew the ruined cities that have been devastated for generations."*
>
> ISAIAH 61:1-4 NIV

The words soaked into my spirit as I drifted off to sleep. I woke up Friday morning with my faith renewed for another day. Good thing too because we headed out for a visit with Slava. I braced myself for a morning with the Tasmanian Devil. The old Looney Toons character seemed a fitting description of our destructive boy.

This time, instead of breakable toys, I brought my trusty secret weapon—bubbles. I blew until the bottle was empty. Slava bounced around trying to catch each iridescent orb. He motioned for Papa to pick him up so he could reach the highest ones. Wayne held him close and prayed while Slava popped. A win-win moment for all. I caught a glimpse of the real little boy inside Slava. A glimmer of hope flickered within me. Maybe we could tame Taz after all.

Our Saturday morning visit went just as well, although the staff sent us outside. Chasing Slava around the frigid playground couldn't cool our excitement though. Missy was scheduled to land in Kyiv that afternoon.

Her arrival provided a huge boost for all of us. A month away from home and family made the trip hardest for Jordan. Big sister lifted little brother's spirit. She also brought him small gifts from home and a big bottle of ranch salad dressing, his favorite dipping sauce.

The next day all four of us smooshed into the backseat of Stanislav's car and headed to Bryankiv. For our first adoption I picked up Andrii and Anna before the mandatory ten-day wait ended. I got Jordan on the tenth day. Six days had now passed since the waiting period for Slava ended. Yet he still remained in the orphanage.

Alexandra kept putting us off when we asked her about picking him up. She warned us Slava might get sick if we removed him from his routine too soon. Different food and interrupted sleep schedule could land him in the hospital. "And we wouldn't want that," she warned.

I suspected Alex feared Wayne and I were no match for little Slava. If we took him too soon, we might change our minds. Maybe she figured we'd give Slava back to the orphanage and flee Ukraine without him. But we were committed to our son and our mission to bring him home.

We didn't pick Slava up from his orphanage until Monday, November 22—a full month after we'd arrived in Ukraine. My journal and my mind pretty much went blank after that. Our busy little boy allowed no time for anything except survival—his and ours.

Within the first hour in our apartment, Slava attempted to destroy everything. He knocked over lamps, unplugged the fridge, switched lights on and off, and flushed the toilet every chance he got.

We tried to contain him to one room. Wayne resorted to sitting guard by the entrance to our main living area. I tried to wrangle Slava while Missy protected Jordan.

All the months leading up to the adoption we assumed the two young brothers would be best buddies. A few hours into the chaos Slava slapped Jordan across the face. Jordan wanted nothing to do with his little brother after that.

For everyone's safety, at bedtime we put Slava in bed between Wayne and me. None of us slept. We were afraid Slava might escape the apartment even with locks on the doors and windows. His tiny body remained rigid all night.

I laid in bed wondering how scared the little boy must be. Slava's traumatized five-year-old brain and body were too immature to process the complexities of adoption. My heart ached for him. While I had no regrets, I wondered how we would all survive.

The next day wasn't any better than the first. And I suspected Slava was swearing at us. He said *peeskah* nonstop. He'd say it with a sly look on his face. We heard him use the word in the orphanage a few times. But now it was the only thing he said.

When we asked Stanislav what it meant, he looked at us with big eyes, shrugged, and shook his head no. I had a feeling our driver did know but didn't want to tell us.

Our missionary friend, Katerina, dropped by the apartment to see how we were doing. Slava looked at her and said, "Peeskah." Kat's hand flew over her mouth. I knew it.

She told us the slang word meant genitals, either male or female. We asked her to explain to Slava that he must not say it anymore. She knelt, made eye contact, and spoke to him in Ukrainian. Slava nodded as if he understood. But he continued to swear.

Part of me felt angry that a little kid, my little kid, swore at me. The other part of me managed to dredge up some empathy. Slava used the word as an attempt to gain some control in his out-of-control world. I understood how he felt.

Tuesday morning Alexandra called with wonderful news—Slava's passport was ready. Relieved, I glanced heavenward and whispered, "Thank you." It took only five days to process counting Saturday and Sunday. We considered the fast turn-around a small miracle.

Two hours later, Stanislav and Alex, drove us to the American Medical Center. Our little Slava passed his mandatory physical. Maybe we would make our flight home after all.

From the clinic, we rode over to the American Embassy—our final step in the adoption process. Jordan remained in the car with the Ukrainian couple and Slava accompanied Wayne and I into the Embassy. We needed to complete immigration paperwork and obtain his Visa. If all went well, we would be on an airplane home the next day. Never mind Slava, I could barely stand still in line. Maybe from the sight of the American flag or the realization we were almost home. Or both. Either way, I was antsy with anticipation.

Another American couple in their forties came into the Embassy right behind us. They were in the process of adopting two teenage sisters. These exhausted parents, whom we learned were from Ohio, looked overwhelmed. Both girls giggled and jumped around as they tickled their adoptive dad with relentless force. He smiled and tried to be playful with them. I could tell he wearied of the game and winced with each tickle. He caught my compassionate smile. "I have bruises all over," he said. I felt sorry for them but had my own powder keg to deal with.

The process at the Embassy seemed to take forever considering we were the only two families waiting. After two hours, the man behind the counter handed me all our documents. We said goodbye to the other adoptive family. I couldn't wait to get back to the apartment and pack. Our 5:30 a.m. flight could not come soon enough.

While we gathered our things to leave, the Embassy's computer system crashed. I heard an officer tell the Ohio family they would have to come back tomorrow. I buried my face in my hands and prayed a silent prayer for them. If the computers had shut down even minutes earlier, we would be in the same position. I thanked God for His divine protection, grabbed Slava's tiny hand, and hustled him out the door.

We arrived at Kyiv's Boryspil International Airport at 3:30 a.m. the next morning. Though still sleepy, Slava wiggled and squirmed. Wayne held him so he couldn't escape. Missy entertained Jordan with her iPod and I managed our tickets and bags. Thirty torturous minutes felt like hours in the security line.

At one point, Slava stretched over my husband's shoulder and whispered, "Peeskah," to the Ukrainian gentlemen in line behind him. Red with embarrassment, I squeezed myself between Slava and the man in line. Excited as I felt to go home, I dreaded the three long flights and layovers ahead.

Our itinerary included short stops in Frankfort, Germany, and Washington D.C. before landing at our final destination—Albany, New York. Waiting to board, I braced myself for twenty-four hours of sleepless travel.

On the airplane I buckled our dynamo into the window seat next to me. Wayne sat across the aisle and Missy and Jordan occupied seats together behind Wayne. I gave Slava a small dose of Benadryl right before takeoff. He didn't even yawn. The flight attendant handed headphones to interested passengers. I placed a pair in Slava's ears. He spent the entire first leg of our journey plugging them in and unplugging them from the jack in the arm rest. I didn't care. It kept him busy.

In Frankfort, Missy and I spent most of the three-hour layover in the women's restroom. We took turns watching Slava stand under the hand dryers. The warm air blowing on his head soothed him.

On the flight from Frankfort to D.C., my eyes zeroed in on the screen molded into the seat in front of me. I watched the tiny airplane icon cross the world map. When we reached the halfway point indicating we were closer to New York than Ukraine, I cried.

Wayne noticed the tears and grabbed my arm. "What did Slava do?"

I shook my head and pointed to the map. Sobbing, I whispered, "We're almost home."

By our layover in Washington, Slava had warmed up to us a little. He let me hold him on my lap and sing him a silly song I'd made up called "Slava La La." The word for baby in Russian sounded like *la la*. The song seemed to resonate with him. So when we weren't chasing Slava around the gate, I'd sing and he'd sit—at least for a few minutes.

We landed in Albany, New York, on November 25, 2010— Thanksgiving Day. Overall, Slava traveled pretty well—much, much better than any of us expected. Our kids and some friends from church welcomed us at the airport. Huddled around the baggage carousel we hugged our welcoming committee and waited for our luggage. With Slava in my arms, I reveled in the reunion. He, however, seemed lost in the sea of strange faces.

I admired the familiar sights on our thirty-minute drive home. But wondered how Slava would adjust to living in a family. We would soon learn that it's easier to take a child out of an orphanage than it is to take the orphanage out of the child.

We walked into our house at 6:00 p.m. to a big Thanksgiving dinner with all the fixings. My mom cooked the feast in my kitchen, so we'd have all the leftovers too. I savored the homecooked holiday meal surrounded by my family and in my favorite place in the whole world—home.

I perched Slava on a stool at our kitchen island and placed a plate in front of him. He didn't care for turkey. But did eat a few spoonfuls of mashed potatoes. The bland taste and texture were probably more akin to his orphanage menu.

Missy swooped in and slipped headphones on Slava's head. Worship music reverberated through his little ears. He rocked back and forth on the stool, absorbed in music and oblivious to the holiday hub bub around him. I watched in awe. Something actually captured Slava's attention for more than a second.

The next morning, Slava appeared in my room at 5:00 a.m. He stood by my bed and demanded, "Manana, kasha, molochko." I dragged my tired self to the kitchen to serve up the requested menu—a banana, oatmeal, and milk.

Neither television nor toys captured Slava's attention. Coloring, Play-Doh, and books didn't interest him. Slava preferred loud music, playing outside, and smashing toys—not my favorite early-morning activities. He offered no compassion for a tired mom who just needed to wake up in a quiet house with a cup of coffee.

The weeks and months blurred together. Slava continued to swear. The more we tried to correct him the more he said *peeskah*. After a while, I tried to ignore it. Maybe if he didn't get a reaction he'd stop. Nope. I introduced new words like *water* and *dog*. Six months passed before Slava's English vocabulary grew enough that he forgot all about the p word.

I searched for tools to help us understand and parent Slava. *The Connected Child* by Dr. Karyn B. Purvis and Dr. David R. Cross became an invaluable resource. "Kids from hard places" is the term Dr. Purvis used to describe foster and adoptive children who have experienced trauma. These children live in a constant state of fear. The human brain's response to fear is fight, flight, or freeze.

Slava never sat still. I recognized fight and flight were his go-to reactions.

The more I learned the more I understood his earliest behaviors were driven by fear. FASD, trauma, and fear were now part of my daily vocabulary. And my education was not over. God was about to teach me some life-changing lessons about orphans and adoption.

CHAPTER 15

God Sets the Lonely in Families

"God sets the lonely in families,
he leads out the prisoners with singing;
But the rebellious live in a sun-scorched land."

PSALM 68:6 NIV

G od planted the seed of adoption in my heart long before I knew it was there. As He nurtured it, I surrendered my heart to His will. The fruit yielded through obedience will forever be my treasure.

Sierra, our third and last biological child, was born on November 24, 1996. By then, Wayne and I were parents of two boys, Wayne Jr., born in 1989, and Curtis, born in 1992. With a baby girl, we believed our family complete.

Six months after Sierra came along, I became pregnant again. The idea of another baby so soon threw me into a panic. Because Sierra suffered from acid reflux, neither she nor I slept much. But after a couple of weeks my head and heart embraced the unexpected blessing. Then I miscarried at eight weeks.

Heartbroken, I found comfort in holding baby Sierra. The miscarriage combined with an infant who never slept and constantly cried led me to a decision—I was done having babies. Wayne and

I agreed, three children completed our family. He had a vasectomy. We were done. But God had other plans.

The same month Sierra was born, my second cousin, Cathy, passed away. She lost her battle with cancer, leaving behind her only child—six-year-old Melissa, whose father had abandoned their family not long after her birth. When Cathy became sick, her mother, my Great Aunt Betty, cared for both mother and child until Cathy died a year later.

Cathy's death added to a list of devastating losses Aunt Betty Link had suffered throughout her life. Back in the Sixties, her teenage son, Peter, died. He was hit by a car while riding a bike on a snowy road days before Christmas. Her husband, Peter Sr., succumbed to cancer in the Seventies. And in 1996, Cathy, her only other child, lost her battle with cancer. Aunt Betty's grief drove her to bitterness. Instead of turning to God for comfort, she turned against Him and everyone around her.

My heart ached because of the tragic losses Melissa and Aunt Betty suffered. Even in the midst of a crying baby and the miscarriage I felt compelled to reach out to them. I extended regular invitations for the pair to come to dinner. Aunt Betty could use the company and Melissa, who now liked to be called Missy, could swim and play with our kids. Aunt Betty called often but only visited on occasion.

The more I reached out to help Aunt Betty the more I realized the little girl was in a bad place. I also realized my great aunt was not healthy. In her early eighties, Betty appeared to have a heart condition. I saw her pop nitroglycerin pills like candy. She summoned me to her house three times because of chest pains, but Aunt Betty always rallied. I knew it only a matter of time before Missy would need a new home.

Melissa lived the life of an old woman. She moved slowly, didn't play outside, stayed up all night watching reruns on Nick at Nite, and missed numerous days of school. Much of what I witnessed disturbed me. I didn't see signs of physical abuse, but Aunt Betty had a twisted way of parenting.

Even more alarming—Aunt Betty appeared mentally unstable. Wayne and I witnessed her emotionally and verbally abuse Missy. She called her "Cathy" all the time—not just a slip of the tongue. Aunt Betty wanted Melissa to be Cathy. She forced the girl to dress and wear her hair the same way Cathy had.

One evening, Aunt Betty called and I could hear Missy crying in the background. "This kid is evil," Betty snapped. Then she screamed at Missy, "I wish you had never been born. You should have died instead of your mother." I grasped the phone and tried to comprehend what I was hearing. How could anyone be so cold-hearted to a child?

Wayne and I had regular discussions about our concerns for Missy's well-being. We hated the way Aunt Betty treated her. Should anything happen, we agreed to open our home to Missy. After all, we were family.

Aunt Betty knew her health was failing. During one visit to our house, she mentioned different people she had visited and listed their good and bad qualities. I read between the lines. My aunt was scouting out future homes for Missy. She knew her days were numbered, and she wanted to be in control of her granddaughter's future.

My aunt never asked Wayne and I if we would take Missy. When I brought it up, she ignored me. Whoever the list of potential candidates were, I got the impression we weren't on it.

In February 1998, Aunt Betty entered the hospital because of heart complications. She left eight-year-old Missy with Mark and Linda Roberts. Missy's mom dated Mark back in high school. Somehow, the Roberts topped Aunt Betty's list of potential parents.

Why my aunt chose Mark and Linda over us baffled me. I met them and their two children. They were nice people. Still, it seemed strange Aunt Betty would choose a long, lost ex-boyfriend over us.

After two weeks in the hospital, Aunt Betty took a turn for the worse. No one expected her to survive. The Roberts filed for temporary custody of Missy. I continued to stay in touch with them. The little girl seemed to be adjusting well. I kept an eye on the situation. I still thought Missy should be with us, but at least for now she was safe and happy.

A month later, Aunt Betty rallied, got out of the hospital and onto the war path. She called me several times a week—always ranting about Mark and Linda. She wanted Missy back. They refused but did permit unsupervised visitations. On several visits, I witnessed my aunt scream at Missy about how horrible the Roberts were. Then the little girl would have to go back to the family at the end of the day. This turn of events perpetuated a long nasty battle between Aunt Betty and Mark and Linda Roberts with a lost little girl caught in between.

I ended up in the middle too. Aunt Betty would call me. I'd call Linda. I knew in my heart it wasn't in Missy's best interest to go back to her grandmother. But the Roberts no longer seemed a viable option either. Aunt Betty's meddling destroyed the earlier bond Missy experienced with them and the situation continued to unravel.

Every week for the next couple months I checked on Missy and prayed God would rescue her from the chaos. Then, Aunt Betty took legal action.

The Roberts were summoned to family court. My aunt asked me to drive her to the courthouse. A week before the court date,

I got calls from both the court appointed law guardian for Melissa and Aunt Betty's lawyer.

Both professionals figured out Aunt Betty had mental health issues. Law guardian, Andrea Bateman questioned why, since I'm a relative, didn't I have custody of Melissa. I explained our willingness and Aunt Betty's unscrupulousness. If we did take Missy, my aunt would destroy the placement just as she had with the Roberts. Everything in me believed Missy belonged with us. At the same time, I knew the second she moved in we would be the target of Aunt Betty's fury.

My aunt's lawyer, Meg Valla, asked for my assessment of the situation. I suggested she might not want to call me as a witness. In good conscience I could not speak in favor of her client.

Tuesday, June 9, 1998, I drove Aunt Betty to family court in Albany, New York. We sat in the waiting room filled with unhappy-looking families. Mark and Linda entered the room. Aunt Betty seethed. She reached into her pocket, pulled out a nitroglycerin tablet, and popped it into her mouth.

When the case was called, we filed into the courtroom along with Betty's lawyer and the law guardian. My stomach churned— this was my first experience in a court of law.

Aunt Betty and her attorney, Meg, sat facing the bench on the right. The Roberts, who hadn't hired a lawyer, took their seats on the left. I settled into the back row and offered up a silent prayer for decisions to be made in Melissa's best interest.

Everyone stood when Honorable Judge Carol Bender entered the courtroom. I raised my eyebrows—she looked like Judge Judy from the TV show. Aunt Betty's lawyer presented opening remarks. Judge Bender asked the Roberts for their side of the story. Aunt Betty had a hard time containing her anger while Mark Roberts spoke.

She shook her head and often made nasty comments under her breath.

Tension in the room escalated. Aunt Betty urged her lawyer to say more. Meg Valla stalled, and Betty grew more agitated. Judge Bender zeroed in on me and peered over her bifocals.

"You're a relative. Would you take custody of the child?"

"Yes."

That one little word made me the new target of Aunt Betty's rage.

Judge Bender asked Andrea Bateman, Missy's law guardian, if she agreed.

"Yes, Your Honor. I believe this decision is in the best interest of the child."

The judge issued a list of orders which flew by me. I tried to grasp what was happening but only caught that I would have temporary custody of Melissa and Aunt Betty was permitted supervised visits.

All parties agreed to Judge Bender's decision—except Aunt Betty of course.

The flurry of activity made me wonder if the lawyers and the judge had a behind-closed-door meeting prior to the formal hearing.

Judge Bender scheduled a follow-up hearing for six weeks later. With a slam of the gavel, I became my aunt's enemy.

Aunt Betty erupted with a slew of hate-filled words for all involved. On her way out of the courtroom, the old woman lunged at her own lawyer.

The law guardian whisked me away to complete some paperwork. While I signed my name to the documents, I marveled at how God had just worked in Missy's behalf.

Thirty minutes later I left court with temporary custody and an irate Aunt Betty. She cursed and berated me all the way to my car. She screamed, stopped to watch which direction I walked, and followed me again still screaming. The few people we encountered just put their heads down and walked by. Maybe this kind of scene was normal in a family court parking lot.

When we reached the car, she ripped open the door. "You just did the worst thing one human being can do to another," she screamed. "You'll get yours. You'll know what it's like to lose someone you love!" She got in and slammed the door.

On the drive home, I remained silent while Aunt Betty ranted. In between threats, she ordered me to deliver Melissa and her toys to her house after school. With a calm voice I reiterated the judge's orders—Missy would be living with me now. Betty fumed.

Twenty minutes later, I dropped her off and drove away. She continued to spew venom from her front steps. I pondered the turn of events. The very act of saying yes in the courtroom had catapulted me onto a battlefield. Aunt Betty may have been an old woman, but she would not give up easily. We were in for a fight. I headed home to warn Wayne.

Aunt Betty appeared on my doorstep two hours later. "I want Melissa and all her toys brought to my house tonight."

"The judge gave me temporary custody of Missy. She will live with us. Her belongings will stay at our house too," I said, surprised at my own restraint.

Aunt Betty shuffled back to her car disgusted, screaming over her shoulder, "You will be hearing from my new lawyer."

My hands shook while I watched her little, white Dodge Neon fly out of our driveway.

Wayne and I knew Aunt Betty would be relentless in her pursuit of Missy. We hired a local attorney that afternoon—Paul Moore, a Christian and an adoptive dad.

Paul lived nearby and stopped at our house on his way home from work. We told him the story of how I obtained custody of Missy that morning. With raised eyebrows he said, "In twenty years of practicing law I have not heard of anything like that happening. It's a miracle Melissa is in your home."

While his words sank in, I realized God was up to something.

Later that evening, Mark and Linda brought Missy and her possessions to our home. She bounced around as we carried her things inside. Missy appeared excited to be moving in with "Aunt Sandra" and "Uncle Wayne." She jumped up and down and clapped her hands at the prospect of sharing a room with three-year-old Sierra.

Missy transitioned well into our family. She relished the outdoors. And spent most of the summer running wild and free on our thirty wooded acres. She learned to swim in our pool, caught frogs in the pond, and went camping with our family. Her first normal childhood experiences since her mom died.

During the next few years, Aunt Betty dragged us to family court three times. The judge saw through her ridiculous accusations. In one she claimed we only allowed her granddaughter to eat cheese and mayonnaise sandwiches. Missy did go through a nasty sandwich phase, but we did not force her to eat them.

Aunt Betty also accused us of being in a cult. She came to that conclusion because we attended church every Sunday morning—at our local Methodist church.

Right from the start, Missy never asked to call or see her grandmother. The initial required visitations were supervised as ordered by family court. Within the first year the judge permitted weekly unsupervised visits. By the second year a once-a-month overnight was allowed. Missy appeared happy yet hesitant about spending time with Betty. While she enjoyed the special attention, she walked on eggshells trying to appease Grandma. But Missy was in her glory at our house—free from her grandmother's control.

Aunt Betty grilled Missy every time they talked. When she called, I put her on speakerphone. She asked Missy what she ate, drank, and how her bowel movements were. Missy appeared uncomfortable with the interrogations and gave brief answers trying to avoid her grandmother's fury. Aunt Betty fished for any information she could twist and use against us in court.

The situation grew volatile by fall 2002. During phone calls, Aunt Betty attempted to manipulate Missy. She would not permit her to use phrases such as *my room* or *my house*. If Missy said, "My shoes are in my room," Aunt Betty lashed out, "Where?" Missy then corrected herself by saying, "My shoes are in the room." Missy was also not allowed to refer to me or Wayne by name when talking with her grandmother. If she used Aunt Sandra and Uncle Wayne, Betty snarled, "Who?" Then Missy had to say they, her, him, or whatever pronoun fit. Aunt Betty tried to tear down every bond we built with Missy.

In November, Aunt Betty sabotaged herself. Her last effort to get even with us and get Missy back ended with court-appointed psychiatric evaluations for Betty, Wayne, Missy, and me. We passed the test. Our lawyer learned Aunt Betty didn't do so well. Her mental state unraveled during her appointment. The incident triggered a health emergency and she ended up in the hospital.

By mid-December compassion got the best of me. Separated for a month, I felt Aunt Betty and Missy should see each other. With Christmas approaching, my conscience compelled me to get them together. I was the last person Aunt Betty wanted to see. So, I asked my friend, Phyllis, to supervise.

Phyllis and Missy visited Betty in the hospital. Missy, now twelve with braces on her teeth, appeared excited to see her grandma.

She dressed in a Christmas sweater and carried a wrapped gift—a framed school picture.

Aunt Betty, however, did not share the holiday spirit. After Missy handed her grandmother the present, she opened it and said, "Did *they* give this to you? Did *they* buy you that sweater?" Missy stood silent when Betty tossed the picture aside. "You betrayed me. Like Judas betrayed Jesus, you betrayed me for the Flachs."

Before Aunt Betty could utter another word, Phyllis grabbed Missy by the hand. They fled the room. In her haste, Phyllis left their coats behind.

At home that afternoon, Missy appeared unscathed by the incident. She trotted off to play American Girl dolls with Sierra before dinner. While tucking her into bed that night, I apologized for her grandmother's behavior. "Grandma is sick. She loves you. She just doesn't know how to show it."

Missy seemed oblivious to the venom her grandmother constantly spewed. Several years would pass before we understood the impact. Missy wasn't oblivious. She was traumatized.

After the hospital visit, our lawyer learned Aunt Betty's health took a turn for the worse. And she was put on suicide watch. The news, while bad for Betty was good for us. Now she would never have a chance to get Missy back. A month later the hospital transferred her to a rehabilitation center an hour away. With Betty's departure, three years of tension dissipated from our lives like a toothache after an extraction.

Five blissful months passed without Aunt Betty's antics. When Mother's Day 2003 neared, we didn't know how much time Betty had left. I felt compelled to arrange another visit between grandmother and granddaughter. Knowing Aunt Betty still despised me, I asked Phyllis to take Missy again. Both put on brave faces and agreed to go.

They found Aunt Betty at the rehab center in a wheelchair, non-verbal and unrecognizable. Years of hatred and anger had destroyed her. Phyllis wheeled Aunt Betty outside for a brief visit in the spring sunshine. She wasn't sure if Betty knew who they were. Missy returned home with a sense of closure. Aunt Betty passed away two weeks later.

The loss of her grandmother caused Missy to worry about the future. That summer, Missy began asking questions. She wondered why her last name was different than ours. She asked if she could still live with us. We assured her no one could take her away from us. I explained that she could have our last name if we adopted her, and we would be happy to adopt her if she wanted us to. It was up to her.

While Aunt Betty was alive, we never discussed adoption with Missy. I knew it would put her in an even more awkward position. With her grandmother gone, Missy was now free to decide if she wanted to be adopted. A few hours after our adoption conversation, Melissa came to me. "I want to be adopted."

Missy became Melissa Elizabeth Flach on May 20, 2004. She became our daughter in the same courtroom and with the same judge who first granted us custody. Judge Bender signed the adoption decree with pleasure. Family and friends joined us to celebrate with a huge party at our house following the formal proceedings.

Little did we know Missy's adoption would be the first of many.

CHAPTER 16

We Didn't Know
What We Didn't Know

"Trust in the LORD with all your heart and lean not on your own understanding; in all your ways submit to him, and he will make your paths straight."

PROVERBS 3:5-6 NIV

O ur adoption journey began more than twenty years ago. We were Bible-believing Christians but not the staunch orphan advocates we are today. Adopting Missy was God's plan. She needed a safe, loving family, parents, and a normal childhood. Wayne and I jumped in with big hearts and both feet. We planned to raise her just like our biological kids with the same opportunities, privileges, and expectations. Then we would all live happily ever after. Our plan, however, didn't go exactly as expected.

Missy was five when she lost her birth mom. We knew Aunt Betty never allowed the little girl to mourn. Missy never met her birth father either. Considering her losses and Betty's harsh treatment, we figured Missy needed some professional help. We arranged counseling for her at different times throughout the years. But a decade passed before we understood the trauma she'd suffered prior to entering our home.

Missy appeared a sweet, bright, happy girl to most. But we experienced her defiant side. Home with the kids all day, I took the brunt of it. While not openly rebellious, Missy wouldn't do simple things I asked her to. Routine tasks became battles. Every day we locked heads over homework and brushing her teeth. When told to clean her room, Missy headed off to comply. Hours later I'd find her sitting in the middle of the mess reading a book. At times I suspected attention deficit disorder.

I struggled always feeling irritated and aggravated by Missy's behavior. I spent most of my time issuing consequences and timeouts. Early bedtimes were my favorite form of discipline. I'd send her to bed early and enjoy a frustration free evening. But Missy never learned from consequences.

With all my energy focused on correcting her behavior, I failed to connect with her heart. I loved her but often found myself not liking her, and I hated myself for it. I prayed for God to help me love her as He did. While I longed for a better relationship with Missy, she ached for her birth mom.

When Missy first joined our family, we never heard about childhood trauma or attachment. The late Dr. Karyn Purvis had not yet developed TBRI (Trust Based Relational Intervention) or written *The Connected Child* with Dr. David Cross. Wayne and I didn't know or understand the impacts of trauma on children. In our desperate attempt to help Slava, we discovered TBRI. Our eyes were opened to a new set of parenting tools designed for parents raising children from hard places. But for the eleven years Missy lived at home, we were uninformed and ill-equipped.

Today, Wayne and I are trauma informed. We trained to become Empowered To Connect parent trainers so we could teach other parents TBRI. Now we understand it takes unconditional love, nurture, and connection to heal hearts. Although Missy is now an adult, we apply TBRI principles whenever we can. Parenting tools such as offering more yesses and finding ways to connect work even with adult kids.

Now we demonstrate unconditional love to our daughter. We have no regrets about adopting Missy. For some reason the Lord saw fit to make us her parents. Missy's story launched our adoption journey.

My only regret—not knowing how to parent a child with a trauma history. It takes a different set of parenting tools to raise kids from hard places. Using the wrong tools can cause additional harm.

Love is necessary. Unconditional love is vital. But love is not enough.

CHAPTER 17

Building our House

"Unless the LORD builds a house,
the work of the builders is useless."

Psalm 127:1 NLT

Wayne and I adjusted to raising four children. Missy fit in
well even with her challenges. She and Sierra shared a
room and became best buddies from the start. The girls paired off
and did everything together—swimming, playing dolls, watching
TV—while our boys, Wayne Jr. and Curtis rode dirt bikes and
skateboards. Even when the kids came together, everyone got along.
Life was good. Little did we know, God had big changes planned for
our family.

All four kids attended a small Christian school not far from
our home. When the doors closed in June 2001, we asked God for
direction. We weren't sure if we should put them in another private
school, send them to public school, or keep them home and teach
them ourselves. After months of praying, we believed the Lord
was leading us to homeschool. That fall, with a sense of fear and
enthusiasm, I began teaching first, fourth, fifth, and sixth grades as
we embarked on what would become a sixteen-year homeschooling
adventure.

The year after we started home educating, God called us to
another big step. For ten years our family attended a local Methodist

church. We loved our pastor and church family, but sensed the Lord leading us in another direction. After meeting with our pastor and spending the summer in prayer, God confirmed the move. In September 2002, with the pastor's blessing, we stepped out in faith and left.

God led us to Gospel Community Church in nearby Coxsackie, New York. This local congregation was filled with large families, many of whom homeschooled. Our kids already had friends at GCC because the homeschool co-op we participated in met there. Our neighbors, Dennis and Lauri Anderson, along with their eight kids, attended Gospel as well. GCC seemed the perfect fit.

The pastor and his wife, Stan and Mary Slager, parented a large crew too. Their three adult children no longer lived home. While empty-nesters, Stan and Mary adopted four siblings from Ukraine in 1999. I loved listening to Pastor Stan share stories about his children from the pulpit. While I marveled at their amazing family, something stirred within me.

During our first year at Gospel Community Church, the Lord began opening my heart to embrace large families, adoption, and a country I knew little about—Ukraine. Back at the Methodist church, we were considered a large family because we had four kids. But at Gospel, several families had eight. Some more. Foster care and adoption were part of the church culture as well. Mission trips to faraway places like Cambodia and Ukraine were annual events. After the first year, I realized that God had positioned us at GCC to prepare us for our next step.

Early 2003, my heart longed for another child. I regretted our vasectomy decision. That hasty choice shut the door to future biological children.

I brought my regret and sorrow to the Lord. He led me to a place of repentance. Wayne and I had taken the matter of life into our own hands. We hadn't prayed or sought God about the vasectomy. We made the decision on our own. Independent of God. Now, filled with remorse, I surrendered my will to God. I wrote these verses in my journal on May 15, 2003:

"A wise woman builds her house;
a foolish woman tears hers down with her own hands."

PROVERBS 14:1 NLT

"A house is built by wisdom and becomes strong through good sense. Through knowledge its rooms are filled with all sorts of precious riches and valuables."

PROVERBS 24:3-4 NLT

"Unless the LORD builds a house,
the work of the builders is useless."

PSALM 127:1 NLT

I decided to trust the Master Builder of our house. Little did I know international adoption would be His divine building plan. Behind the scenes, God worked to prepare our family. He positioned us in the place where we would hear and heed His call to adopt again.

Throughout the summer I prayed, read my Bible, and journaled. I observed my friend Phyllis with her two children—one adopted domestically and one from Russia. Everywhere I turned something about adoption popped up. My mom, whom I hadn't shared my heart with yet, handed me a newspaper article about a local family who'd adopted twins internationally. And Pastor Stan seemed to weave stories about his Ukrainian kids into every sermon.

By August, I recognized the stirring in my heart was the Lord calling us to adopt. I surrendered. Yes, Lord, we will grow our family through adoption. But what about Wayne? Would he be on board?

Up to this point, all my conversations about adoption were between me and God. I'd never mentioned anything to Wayne. We enjoyed a great marriage. He was a wonderful dad. But there was a distance between us. It felt as if we were not on the same page. Our construction business occupied much of his time. He seemed more interested in motorcycles and snowmobiles than in growing our family. I wondered how my husband would respond to such a life changing call from God.

Before I could utter a word about adoption to Wayne, the Lord issued a warning: "You are not the Holy Spirit for your husband." Then He issued my first assignment—pray and wait for God to move.

Keeping my mouth shut took immense effort. I fought the temptation to use the power of persistent persuasion. If God called me to adopt, then He called both of us. Wayne needed to hear from God for himself. Tug-of-war with the Lord became a regular game. Trust, doubt, trust, doubt, trust. I trusted God to move in Wayne's heart. Then gave Him reasons why Wayne would never agree to adopt. One reason I often pointed out—our house wasn't big enough.

We built our three-bedroom home in 1989. And filled it with two parents and four kids. Wayne Jr. and Curtis shared a room. Missy and Sierra shared a room. There were no more rooms and no more room in the rooms we had.

Our log home haven was set on thirty wooded acres complete with a pond and pool. We'd built a sanctuary in the country perfect for raising a family. Moving was out of the question. And I felt certain Wayne wouldn't go for building an addition either.

In late August, Isaiah 54 popped up in my morning devotions:

"Enlarge the place of thy tent, and let them stretch forth the curtains of thine habitations: spare not, lengthen thy cords, and strengthen thy stakes; For thou shalt break forth on the right hand and on the left; and thy seed shall inherit the Gentiles, and make the desolate cities to be inhabited."

ISAIAH 54:2-3 KJV

Through these scriptures God assured me that He would enlarge our house. I surrendered. The Lord won the tug-of-war. But I still wondered how He would get a hold of Wayne.

On Labor Day 2003, Wayne and I sat together on the porch enjoying our morning coffee. God nudged me. I spilled my heart to my husband. My nerves tried to get the best of me. But with calm and reason, I laid out everything the Lord showed me: the biblical mandate in James 1:27, our resources of time, money, home, and love, and Pastor Stan and Mary's example of adoption. I closed my case with the declaration, "I believe God is calling us to adopt from Ukraine too."

Wayne listened without saying a word. I could tell he was trying to process my presentation. By the time I finished, a look of stunned panic had settled over him. After several silent minutes he responded. "I see what you're saying. Maybe we can look into it when our kids are older."

Not the response I hoped for. Fending off disappointment, I shook my head. "I believe God is calling us to adopt now. He is calling both of us, not just me." I pleaded, "Please pray about it."

Wayne agreed to pray.

My next assignment from the Lord—be quiet, pray, and wait. Again, not easy. But I wanted Wayne to hear from the Lord for himself. We both needed to be positive God was calling us. What if we adopted and it ended in disaster? I didn't want Wayne blaming me for havoc wreaked on our family. Adoption is a serious matter requiring parental unity. I chose to be obedient and wait for the Holy Spirit to unify us.

Over the next several months, the Lord continued to speak through His Word. Matthew 25 in particular stood out. God drew me to the three servants in verses 14-29. In the parable a man goes away and entrusts his servants with money. To one servant he gave five bags of gold, to another two bags, and the third servant was given one bag. The first two servants went out and invested the gold and doubled their investment. But the third servant buried his gold in the earth.

After a time, their master returned from his trip. He called his servants together to give an account of how they used their gifts. The master praised the two servants who increased their investment. He said to both, "Well done, my good and faithful servant. You have been faithful in handling this small amount, so now I will give you many more responsibilities. Let's celebrate together!" But the servant who played it safe didn't fare so well. He buried his gold in the earth, too afraid to use it. The master took the small amount away from this servant and had him thrown into outer darkness.

These verses solidified in my heart. God gives every believer talents—gifts to invest in His Kingdom. We are not to plant our gifts into selfish pursuits. Western Christians are often distracted by the American Dream. We chase after what we think is the good life, but along the way lose sight of the greater life God has for us. What are we living for? Are we investing our God-given gifts back into His Kingdom? Are we living for ourselves or for Jesus?

There is no greater affirmation from the Lord than hearing, "Well done good and faithful servant." I began to see adoption as a Kingdom investment. And investing into the lives of children as one of the reasons God entrusted us with our plentiful resources.

Wayne ran a successful business. I loved being a stay-at-home mom. We owned our house and had a decent amount of money in the bank. We lived a comfortable life. It's not wrong to enjoy what we earn. But the Lord opened my eyes. Our blessings were given for a greater purpose. One that reaped a higher reward. An eternal reward.

In December 2003, our family attended a special church service. An area pastor shared about his recent mission trip to Ukraine. The pastor and his team had just returned from the YWAM base in Kyiv where Pastor Stan's daughter, Laura, served. Orphans were the main focus of his message. I spent the entire evening captivated by pictures and stories of orphaned children. Wayne sat next to me. I prayed God would open his ears and heart. All the while I kept my arms folded and glued to my middle so I wouldn't jab my elbow into his ribs. Instead, I waited for the Lord to do the jabbing—which seemed to take forever.

On Mother's Day 2004, Wayne and I sat together in church. Nine months had passed since our first and only conversation about adoption. Pastor Stan spoke about the most important ministry—motherhood. He wove stories about his adopted children throughout the sermon. I felt certain Wayne could hear my heart pounding. Pastor ended with, "Not everyone is called to adopt. But every family should pray about it."

My elbow made contact with Wayne's ribs.

A few days later, we were in our bedroom putting away laundry and chatting about yardwork, opening the pool, and pretty much everything other than what I wanted to talk about. Unable to stand the silence on the subject any longer, I asked Wayne what he thought of the Mother's Day message from Pastor Stan.

"It was good."

Good? I wanted to hear more than *good*. I tossed a stack of jeans onto a shelf in our walk-in closet and tried to sound calm.

"You promised to pray about adoption. So, what is God telling you?"

My husband shoved socks into a drawer before confessing. "I haven't prayed about it."

With my back to Wayne and my face in the closet, I begged God for the right response. I could have flipped out, cried, gotten offended, or any number of other manipulative reactions. But there in my closet, I heard God's still, small voice. *Wayne hasn't prayed about it because he's afraid of the answer.*

Hurt and discouragement threatened to steal my composure. Taking a deep breath, I backed out of the closet and faced my husband. "Nothing has changed. I still believe God is calling us to adopt." I swallowed and tried hard not to sound indignant. "Please pray about it."

Wayne slid the dresser draw closed. "Okay." Then he headed out the bedroom door.

I sat on the edge of our bed and watched him out the window. He zig-zagged around our yard on a riding lawnmower. I sighed. Mowing the lawn would be a great time to pray about adoption. Collapsing back on my pillow, I prayed. "God, help me have a right attitude."

CHAPTER 18

Getting on the Same Page

" . . . the effective, fervent prayer
of a righteous man avails much."

JAMES 5:16 NKJV

A few weeks later, Wayne and I attended a cookout at the home of Dennis and Lauri Anderson. Other families from our church were invited, along with Laura and Joey Stoltzfus—the missionary couple home from Ukraine on furlough. Over burgers and potato salad, the conversation buzzed with stories about Ukraine and orphans. I soaked up every bit of information but kept silent.

My friend Lauri peppered the talk with questions about adoption. She knew my heart. I must have driven her crazy almost every day for months on this subject. Lauri was the only other person I could bare my soul to about adoption. She did her part to make sure my husband got the message.

Wayne enjoyed the fellowship but maintained a poker face. I couldn't tell if or how the discussion affected him. I engaged in the chitchat while pleading silent prayers, begging God to touch my husband's heart.

Though I couldn't see it, God worked behind the scenes. The following month, July 2004, Wayne and Wayne Jr., now fifteen, went on a two-week mission trip to Cambodia. The overseas adventure with a team from our church was a first for both father and son.

My husband came home impacted to his core. It took weeks to process everything he experienced in Cambodia. The killing fields of Khmer Rouge, abject poverty, and countless street children haunted his thoughts. A bit of hope flickered within me. I prayed Wayne's sleepless nights were a sign God was breaking through.

Three months later, Missy, now fourteen, and I made our first overseas trip. We spent two weeks in Kyiv, Ukraine, with a group from church. Orphans were the focus of our mission and James 1:27 the theme verse. I had an ulterior motive—to obtain definitive confirmation. I needed to know if the Lord was truly calling us to adopt from Ukraine. Tired of dreaming and desperate for things to move forward, I believed this trip would yield answers.

God did not disappoint.

God Speaks Through People

Our first Sunday in Ukraine, we attended a Russian-speaking church. The pastor preached from Luke 10. Even through the hushed whispers of our translator his message captivated me. I recorded his words in my journal. "Jesus told them the harvest is ready but there are not enough workers. We must stop excuses. God is waiting for you. Pray to the God of the harvest. When God shows you something, you must answer. So often we worry about what will happen next. Don't worry. Do it now. God calls. He equips. Let your excuses die and your dedication come."

The pastor's sermon began to solidify adoption in my heart.

Our team attended a Family Night event at the YWAM base. This time a pastor from Washington State spoke. He used Acts 14:8-10 about a man crippled from birth who had been healed by Paul. Then the pastor shared a story about how he and his wife were asked to take in three teenagers. His wife said yes right away, but his first reaction—no way, I can't do that.

The pastor explained, "Like the cripple in Acts 14, we are all 'crippled' at birth. But Jesus came and adopted us. In Acts 14 the people of Lystra thought Paul and Barnabas were gods, but Paul declared they were only ordinary men. God uses ordinary people. The crippled who cross our path need us. God needs ordinary people who absolutely trust an extraordinary God."

Through a Washington pastor speaking in Ukraine, God showed this ordinary girl that she needed to trust her extraordinary God.

Early the next morning I awoke with Matthew 25 running through my mind. I wondered if the Lord had another message for me. Maybe it was just my imagination or maybe I wanted to hear what I wanted to hear. Desperate for guidance, I randomly opened my Bible. Matthew 25 displayed on the pages before me.

I read again about the master who entrusted his servants with bags of gold. Two servants demonstrated faithfulness and obedience with the gifts their master had given. In turn, the master multiplied their gifts. I meditated on these verses.

Wayne and I desired to be faithful and obedient too. We worked hard to raise our four children for the Lord. Maybe God planned to bless us with more. Maybe He wanted to multiply our gifts by entrusting us with more children.

I grabbed my journal and recorded the following verses from Matthew:

"To those who use well what they are given,
even more will be given, and they will have an abundance."
MATTHEW 25:29 NLT

*". . . I assure you, when you did it to one of the least of these
my brothers and sisters, you were doing it to me."*

MATTHEW 25:40 NLT

*"And anyone who welcomes a little child
like this on my behalf is welcoming me."*

MATTHEW 18:5 NLT

On our team's last Sunday in Ukraine, we attended International Christian Assembly, an English-speaking Assemblies of God church in Kyiv. The pastor announced the title and text of his message—"Digging Up Your Treasure and Planting it in the Kingdom of God" from Matthew 25:14-30. He owned my full attention.

"We all have something to offer to the Lord. We must join forces with His purposes and invest in the Kingdom of God." He ended with a warning. "If we hold back our time, our resources, or our lives, we will miss the blessing God has for us."

My pen flew across the pages of my journal. I tried to catch every word the pastor spoke. Throughout those two weeks in Ukraine, my little notebook became a chronicle of God's call for us to adopt. I ached for Wayne to hear these messages of confirmation from the Lord.

God Speaks Through Experiences

I stepped into an orphanage for the first time on October 4, 2004. Our team traveled over an hour outside Kyiv by bus and train to the village of Vorzel. When we arrived, the orphanage director sent us outside. We spent two hours in the chilly autumn air playing with preschool-aged orphans.

The children, stuffed into snow suits and winter hats, waddled around the yard laughing. Our team of eight women pushed the bundled babies on rickety swings, helped them climb ancient monkey bars, and chased them around the dreary playground.

I paired up with a little blond boy named Rostyk. When I reached out my hand, much to my delight, the little three-year-old grabbed it and led me to the swings. My heart soared as he giggled at the silly sounds I made with each push.

The highlight for me that day, however, came when I met Kareel. The tiny, five-year-old was born with a cranial-facial deformity known as Treacher-Collins Syndrome. But Kareel's personality outshined his deformities. Our team nicknamed him Mayor because he seemed to run the show. Despite his appearance, Kareel displayed leadership skills. The other children looked to him for help getting their coats on and shoes tied for our trip to the playground.

We knew something Kareel didn't—despite his need for multiple surgeries, a family waited for him. After Laura, Pastor Stan's daughter, advocated for Kareel to be adopted, her own parents felt compelled to respond. The Slagers were only weeks away from finalizing paperwork.

During our third visit to Vorzel, a little girl took my hand and stole my heart. Three-year-old Natasha with her brown hair, dark eyes, and chubby cheeks held my hand while we walked around the playground. She reached out for me to pick her up. Love engulfed my heart. I sought her out whenever we visited the orphanage. During the rest of the trip, I wondered if she could be my daughter.

Longing to know if Natasha was available for adoption, I asked our translator, Dima, if he could find out for me. Dima met with the orphanage director and learned, yes, Natasha was freed for adoption. My hands shook and my heart raced. Natasha could be the child God called us to adopt.

Our mission team traveled to Vorzel a half-dozen times. Each visit solidified adoption in my heart and mind. I spent the long bus and train rides to and from the orphanage praying. And I recorded Isaiah 52:6 (NLT) in my journal: "But I will reveal my name to my people, and they will come to know its power. Then at last they will recognize that it is I who speaks to them." Everything within me knew God was speaking. I begged Him to open Wayne's ears so he could hear too.

After a week of visits to Vorzel, Dima took our team to a private Christian orphanage. The facility consisted of eight buildings on twelve acres just outside Kyiv. An American couple, Jim and Diane, established and ran the orphanage. Many of the children there were street kids and runaways from government orphanages.

Diane told us God worked a miracle for them to obtain this prime property. Jim and Diane's story showed me God can make a way where there seems to be none—a message my faith desperately needed to embrace.

Later that night, Wayne and I talked by phone—our first real conversation since I'd arrived in Ukraine. I missed my husband and yearned to share my heart but struggled to find words. Careful to not bulldoze him over with my emotions, I did muster up the courage to ask if he prayed about adoption at all.

Wayne confessed he had prayed *a little*. After the call I curled up on the bed in our team's rental apartment. I fell asleep praying Wayne would hear from God *a lot*.

Our team returned home mid-October 2004. I relished being with my family, but anxiety filled my gut. Wayne seemed distant.

We barely spoke and when we did, I chose my words with caution. I feared if I opened up, the dam would break, and he'd drown in my emotions. Pregnant with the experience from the trip, I ached to pour it all out to him. I didn't know how to hold it in any longer. Yet, I didn't feel free to bare my soul to my own husband. What if I said the wrong thing? What if his answer was a definitive no?

A few days later, the dam gave way. While Wayne dressed for work, I sat on the edge of our bed and fell apart. Through tears I begged him to talk to me. He explained he'd been under a lot of stress at work and wasn't sure how to handle it. I didn't want to add more to his load before he left for the day and chose not to dump everything on him at that moment. Before he left, I said, "We're both unhappy. We're not on the same page. Something needs to change." My words seemed to soak in. He nodded, gave me a hurried hug, and headed out our bedroom door.

Two days later, I sat in our living room for my morning quiet time. With my Bible open on my lap and a hot cup of coffee warming my hands, the unexpected sound of Wayne's truck roused me from prayer. He walked in and sat beside me on the couch. I moved my Bible and coffee to the end table. He'd captured my full attention.

Wayne opened up about the stress at work, something he tried to leave at the job but always came home on his shoulders. Navigating the fine line between too much work and not enough good workers and too little work to keep his men employed was a constant struggle.

After apologizing for being distant, Wayne asked me to share my heart. With his permission, I poured out everything the Lord showed me. I handed him the photo album from my trip. I pointed out all the pictures of orphans, including Natasha. He looked over my journal and all the scriptures. I told him God spoke loud and clear—we are called to adopt from Ukraine.

My husband sat on our couch with my journal on his lap. After a few silent minutes he said, "Adoption is the right thing to do. We will probably do it. I just really need to hear from the Lord on it."

Ugh. Okay. But I'd heard all I needed to hear from the Lord. More than a year passed since that Labor Day morning I first brought up adoption. I spent fourteen months waiting for Wayne to hear from God. How much longer before he gets the message? I considered buying the man some hearing aids.

While I continued to wait for Wayne to hear from the Lord, my heart ached for the orphans in Ukraine, especially Natasha. She consumed my thoughts and dreams. I imagined her playing in our yard, in the nursery at church, and on my lap as I read to her.

In early November, driven by impatience and the need to do something, I sewed a fleece blanket and sent it to Ukraine. Dima promised to deliver it to Natasha. I asked him to inquire if she had siblings. While I longed for Natasha to be our daughter, I also had an unexplainable sense we were to adopt a sibling group. In the meantime, her photo hung on our refrigerator—a picture of my heart. Wayne saw the little face on our fridge every day but never said anything. I prayed God would use Natasha to soften his heart.

A month later, doubt set in. Did this call to adopt exist only in my head? Wayne remained mute on the subject. I poured over my journals and reread the scriptures. My heart's cry—to be consumed by what consumes God. Orphans and adoption swallowed me whole. In tears I begged the Lord for a sign. Then journaled these verses:

". . . the effective, fervent prayer of a righteous man avails much."
JAMES 5:16 NKJV

"Ask, and it will be given to you; seek, and you will find; knock, and it will be opened to you. For everyone who asks receives, and he who seeks finds, and to him who knocks it will be opened."

Matthew 7:7-8 NKJV

"Take delight in the Lord, and He will give you your heart's desires."

Psalm 37:4 NLT

A few days later Lauri and Dennis Anderson came over for a visit. Over day-old Thanksgiving pie, Lauri asked Wayne if he planned to go to Cambodia again, a trip our church had announced for the next summer. With his head in the fridge digging around for whipped cream he answered. "No, we might be in Ukraine at that time."

I almost dropped my pie.

Later that night after our company left, Wayne and I snuggled on our living room couch. My heart soared. It had taken over a year, but God answered my prayers. We were finally on the same page. Now we needed to know our next step. Before heading to bed, Wayne and I held hands and prayed for direction.

CHAPTER 19

Caught Unarmed

*"Therefore, put on every piece of God's armor so you will be
able to resist the enemy in the time of evil. Then after the
battle you will still be standing firm."*

Ephesians 6:13 NLT

A few days later, I received an email from Dima. Natasha did
not have siblings. I had been wondering and praying if we
were supposed to adopt her. Or maybe God only used Natasha to
get through to Wayne. As much as the little girl touched my heart,
we needed to be sure. I couldn't get over the feeling that we are
supposed to adopt siblings not just a single child. And something
was telling me Natasha wasn't ours. Before bed that night we prayed
together again asking God for clarity.

During my quiet time one December morning I saw a vision in
which Wayne and I walked with the Lord. We were surrounded by
light and full of joy. Then terrible darkness swallowed us. The vision
ended. I opened my eyes and shivered. Not sure what to do next,
I opened my Bible. God led me to Isaiah 60:1-5 NLT.

*"Arise, Jerusalem! Let your light shine for all nations to see! For
the glory of the Lord is shining upon you. Darkness as black as
night will cover all the nations of the earth, but the glory of the
Lord will shine over you. All nations will come to your light.
Mighty kings will come to see your radiance. Look and see, for*

everyone is coming home! Your sons are coming from distant lands; your little daughters will be carried home. Your eyes will shine, and your hearts will thrill with joy, for merchants from around the world will come to you. They will bring you the wealth of many lands."

Sitting there on my couch God's presence overwhelmed me. He spoke to me through His Word as He often did. He assured me, darkness might appear on our adoption journey, but the Lord promised to shine His light over us. I clung to the Scripture believing our sons and daughters, the wealth of the nations, would come home.

By the end of December, Wayne and I reached a decision. One that would change our lives. One we hoped would be for the best. As soon as the holidays were over, we'd contact the Christian adoption agency Pastor Stan and Mary used—Reaching Arms International. Because international adoption is risky, we wanted a tried-and-true agency.

Reaching Arms International no longer exists. I recommend anyone considering international adoption visit the Christian Alliance For Orphans website at cafo.org. There you will find a list of reputable adoption agencies.

On January 2, 2005, I poured a huge cup of coffee, sat at the kitchen table, and dove into a mountain of adoption paperwork. With intimidation and excitement, I looked over the document checklist our agency provided. Adoption applications, background checks, medical forms, home study, copies of our marriage license, birth certificates, passports, bank statements, employment status forms, tax returns—all of which needed to be notarized, county certified, and stamped with a state apostille. Once complete, our dossier would be sent to Ukraine, translated, and submitted to the government for approval.

The looming list would take months to complete. I'm a procrastinator when it comes to routine paperwork, checkbook balancing, and such. But, knowing the sooner this paperwork was finished meant the sooner we could travel to Ukraine and adopt our kids. I resolved to get this monumental task done in record time. I gulped some coffee, picked up my pen, and tackled the first form.

By early spring, I neared the bottom of the paperwork pile. With the finish line in sight, my focus zeroed in on the final steps. Distracted by my to-do list, I didn't see the enemy positioned to attack.

The darkness God warned about rolled in when we attempted to complete two key parts of our dossier. First, our Form I-600A needed to be submitted at the Bureau of Citizenship and Immigration Service (BCIS). This application included an FBI background check and would determine if we were found suitable and eligible to adopt internationally. Second, we had to meet with our social worker, Rachael, for our home study. I decided to check both boxes off our list on the same day.

On a chilly Thursday afternoon in March, I strutted through the doors of BCIS with Wayne behind me. We stepped into the security line at 2:03 p.m. A gruff federal officer poked through the contents of my purse. "What business are you here for today?"

His crabby demeanor could not squash my enthusiasm. "We're here to file our I-600A for an international adoption."

"You're too late."

The officer's emotionless declaration annoyed me. I knew how to tell time. "The office is open until 3:00 p.m. It's only a few minutes past two." I punctuated my response with a smile.

The man shook his head and pointed to a sign above the window we needed to visit. I looked up. Closed. Although the BCIS office was open until 3:00 p.m., the department we needed closed at 2:00 p.m.

Deciding a federal security officer was not someone to argue with, I snatched up my purse and our documents and headed back out the door. Wayne didn't say much, but the aggravation triggered me into a rant about government bureaucracy. I had checked the BCIS website prior to making arrangements for Wayne to leave work early. Nothing indicated any part of the office closed at 2:00 p.m. Now we had three hours to kill before our meeting with Rachael.

Wayne drove to a nearby seafood restaurant—one of our favorites. I picked at my entree, not in the mood for small talk or shrimp scampi. Finishing the paperwork and adopting our kids were the only things I cared about. We set out that afternoon to accomplish one of the most important parts of the process. Instead, aggravation inched my blood pressure higher as I poked a tiny sea creature around my plate.

Wayne tried to be encouraging. "We'll just try again next week."

I sighed, stabbed a shrimp, and popped it into my mouth.

After dinner we drove a few miles up the road to our meeting with Rachael. When we arrived, her office looked dark and empty. A man leaving the building told us she should be back around 5:30 p.m. Wayne and I sat outside in his truck and waited. He passed the time making calls for work. I watched every car drive by and not pull into the parking lot. Where was Rachael? She scheduled this meeting.

At 6:00 p.m. my cell rang. I pounced on the phone when I saw Rachael's number on the screen. "Where are you?" she asked. "Are you coming for the meeting?"

"What? We've been sitting in the parking lot outside your office for an hour." My face burned. I could feel my blood pressure and panic rising in me.

"Are you at the Clifton Park office?"

"Yes. We've been waiting here for an hour."

"Ah, I'm so sorry. On Tuesdays and Thursdays I work from the Albany office. How fast can you get here? We might be able to start the interview, but we won't have enough time to finish it."

You've got to be kidding me? How could this be happening? Through tears I wrote down the address for the Albany office. I hung up the phone unable to hold back the expletive that escaped my mouth. I threw the pen on the floor and flung the directions to Wayne in the driver's seat.

Twenty minutes later we arrived at the Albany location. Rachael, an attractive middle-aged woman with a stunning smile, greeted us at the door. I tried to smile back, but my red puffy eyes gave away my mood. Rachael apologized again for the misunderstanding. She put her hand on my shoulder and with compassion whispered, "I heard what you said when you hung up the phone."

I burst into tears. All the frustration from the afternoon spilled out right there in front of our social worker. Wayne put his arm around me. I buried my face in my hands. Embarrassment flushed my cheeks. Two years earlier, Rachael had conducted our home study for Missy's adoption. She knew we are a Christian family. And now she must have thought I was a fake.

"It was out of character for you. You must have had a horrible day."

Her empathy helped me feel a tiny bit better.

With thirty minutes left to spend with us, Rachael handed me some forms and scheduled the mandatory home visit. Because of the previous adoption, our home study only needed to be updated. An update was not as tedious as the initial evaluation. She assured us it wouldn't take long.

Back in the truck I released a long groan—mortified at my own behavior. Though grateful something got accomplished, anger stirred in me at the blatant roadblocks in our path. I recognized enemy opposition and hated how powerless I felt. In a rush to meet Wayne at work and get to BCIS, we never took time to pray. Lesson learned. I took note: spiritual armor was essential when fighting spiritual battles.

"A final word: Be strong with the Lord's mighty power. Put on all of God's armor so that you will be able to stand firm against all the strategies and tricks of the devil. For we are not fighting against people made of flesh and blood, but against the evil rulers and authorities of the unseen world, against mighty powers in this dark world, and against spirits in the heavenly places. Therefore, put on every piece of God's armor so that you will be able to resist the enemy in the time of evil. Then after the battle you will still be standing firm."

EPHESIANS 6:10-13 NLT

CHAPTER 20

My Heart's Desire

"Take delight in the LORD, and he will give you your heart's
desires. Commit everything you do to the LORD.
Trust him, and he will help you."

PSALM 37:4-5 NLT

By the end of March, I mailed our adoption dossier to Reaching Arms in Minnesota. Walking out of the post office I felt like Rocky Balboa running up the cement steps in Philly. Completing three months of appointments and paperwork brought us one step closer to Natasha—or whomever we were to adopt. The agency discovered the little girl would be available for adoption sometime in August. We hoped the timing worked out if she was to be our daughter.

Reaching Arms sent our dossier off to Andrew Parker in Ukraine. Andrew's team needed to translate every document and deliver the dossier to the State Department for Adoption (SDA) in Kyiv. The SDA would review the documents and approve or deny us permission to adopt. So here we were again—waiting. I counted the days and prayed God would escort our dossier every step of the way.

In mid-July, standing in the kitchen prepping a salad for dinner, my phone rang. Julia, a Russian woman who worked for Reaching Arms, called with news. "Your dossier has been denied."

What? My heart sank to my feet. I grabbed the counter for support. Julia explained the agency didn't know the reason for the denial yet. She promised to call as soon as they knew anything more. With trembling hands, I hung up the phone and managed to utter seven desperate words, "Oh God, you've got to fix this."

While we waited for more information from the agency, Wayne and I discussed building an addition onto our home. The excitement of a renovation project helped distract me from the dossier dilemma. The adoption never left my thoughts, but planning new rooms provided a positive outlet for my restless energy.

Around the same time, I learned some disturbing news from our agency—Ukraine might be suspending their adoption program temporarily. The supposed closure, for reorganization purposes, held no guarantee for if or when the program would reopen. Our adoption agency took a wait-and-see stance. But with our dossier in limbo, the weight of the wait felt like an hourglass on my shoulders. I watched powerlessly as grains of sand filled the bottom.

Throughout the summer I could not shake the sense we were to adopt more than one child. Our dossier already included duplicate sets of documents—a strategy typical for international adoption. If a family chooses a child who turns out to have a sibling, the extra paperwork was already complete.

Every morning I stared at Natasha's picture on our fridge. She had no brothers or sisters. The little girl tugged at my heart, yet a compelling force pulled me toward a sibling group. I continued to pray for a definitive answer.

After waiting two weeks, Julia finally called to report the problem with our paperwork. "Ukraine does not like the wording on some of your documents. The medical report from your doctor must be redone. And she must use blue ink."

You've got to be kidding me. Even though I passed my physical and the required blood work, we were rejected because the doctor used black ink and the wrong words? Asking Dr. Atkins to hand write the entire report the first time felt awkward enough. Now I had to ask her to do it over and tell her what to write.

Annoyed, I scheduled an appointment for the following week. This time our agency provided a script for the doctor to follow. I handed her a blue pen and watched while she spent thirty minutes filling out the duplicate documents. When the doctor finished, I thanked her for her patience. She seemed happy to help, but I grew weary of jumping through ridiculous hoops.

After the new forms were notarized, sealed, and apostilled, I overnighted them to Reaching Arms in Minnesota. Then the agency sent them to Ukraine for translation and resubmission. With our dossier corrected the waiting game resumed. I returned to praying and crossing days off the calendar.

One morning in late August, the phone rang. From the shower, I grabbed the cordless phone that stayed within my reach every minute of every day while I waited for *the* call to come. Shampoo dripped on the floor as I listened to Julia's words. "Your dossier is approved. You will receive an appointment letter from Ukraine. Let us know when it arrives."

Woohoo! Praise the Lord! I hung up and danced a jig right there in the shower.

Before my hair dried, I assumed my post watching for the mailman. Like an eagle I eyeballed every delivery truck in my neighborhood. The letter would inform us of our appointment with the SDA. We could not make travel plans until we knew the date we needed to be in Kyiv. This piece of paper was the only hurdle between us and our kids. I anticipated its arrival every day—for weeks.

The letter from Ukraine finally arrived in November, almost eight weeks after Julia's call. But it was not an invitation to travel. Instead, the letter informed us all adoption appointments were filled for 2005. Ukraine postponed issuing appointments to approved families until January 2006.

I sat in my car packed with Thanksgiving groceries and read the letter over and over. More waiting? A normal pregnancy lasts forty weeks. The gestational period for an elephant is two years. We were in elephant territory and I did not like it one bit.

Wayne arrived home from work. I showed him the letter when we sat down for dinner.

He read it and handed it back. "Let's be optimistic," he said. "Focus on the holidays. We'll probably travel the beginning of the new year."

Nodding, I swallowed a spoonful of soup. Images of a snow-covered village captured my imagination. I made a note to purchase winter coats for Christmas. And luggage. If I had to wait, I'd make the best of it.

In late January, I sat at our kitchen table going over math problems with one of our kids. The phone rang. When I heard Julia's voice, I jumped like a kid ready to pounce into birthday presents.

"The rumors are true. Ukraine closed its adoption program." Her sober words felt like a gut punch. "They promise to reopen. When they do, appointment dates will be issued according to registration numbers. I am sorry."

I collapsed back onto the kitchen chair. "Julia, how long will it take them to reorganize?" She offered no answer. Her only advice—wait.

To pass the time, I poured myself into praying, reading adoption books, and my newest obsession—visiting the Families for

Ukrainian and Russian Adoption (FRUA) chat room. Every day I lost myself in this virtual room full of real families who either already adopted from Ukraine or were in the process, like us. The former group offered tips on where to eat, what to pack, and what to do while in Ukraine. Those of us in the latter group tried to encourage each other through the waiting process.

On days when doubt set in, God's Word and my journals brought comfort. Each reminded me that I had heard from the Lord about adoption. I also spent time reminding God of His own Words.

God, you said you are the Father of the fatherless. You said you put the lonely in families. You called us to care for orphans and widows— that's what we are trying to do, Lord. But we can't do it unless you open the door to Ukraine. Open the door, God.

Desperate people pray bold prayers.

By spring 2005, our agency connected me with a Minnesota mom also waiting to adopt from Ukraine. Staci and I talked on the phone and prayed together every week. From my porch in New York and Staci's in Minnesota, we stormed the gates of heaven for orphans in Ukraine. We were the only people in each other's lives who understood the grueling wait.

One evening in April, Mary, our pastor's wife, called with news—Natasha had been adopted by a Ukrainian family. Laura had contacted Mary from Ukraine. She asked her mom to break the news to me. While her startling words sank in a sudden peace settled over me. The women expected me to be crushed by the virtual loss of a child who was never mine. Instead, I rejoiced. Natasha got a family and I got confirmation.

May arrived with a call from Julia. I loved hearing her Russian accent on the phone but hated the news she delivered. "Your documents are expiring. You must do them all again."

Julia sounded apologetic. It wasn't her fault. It wasn't the agency's fault. It wasn't my fault—but I had to pay the price. I scribbled her instructions across my grocery list and hung up. A full-on temper tantrum simmered within.

I ran out of the house slamming the porch door behind me. My feet pounded the pavement as I complained to God about the injustice of it all. One year and thousands of dollars into the adoption process and we still had nothing to show for it. Now all our documents are expiring. Everything had to be redone. Everything.

A quarter of a mile down our dead-end country road a knowing settled into my heart. Redoing our dossier presented the opportunity to increase the number of children we requested to adopt. Our original paperwork specified two children in case Natasha had a sibling. Now we could apply for a sibling group of three or four. I turned and pranced back to the house, marveling at how God worked behind the scenes.

Later that day, laughter and barbeque smoke mingled together in the afternoon sun. Our kids splashed in the pool while I grilled hamburgers for dinner. Lifting the lid to check the burgers, I heard Wayne's truck pull up the driveway. He strolled through the yard, lunchbox in hand, and stopped to plant a kiss on my forehead. I flipped the burgers and filled him in on the adoption news. He listened when I explained my frustrations with climbing the paperwork mountain again. I closed the grill and faced my husband. "Since I have to redo all the paperwork, I believe we should apply to adopt four children."

Wayne got that deer-in-the-headlights look on his face. "I don't know, San. That's a lot."

Four didn't seem far-fetched to me. The Slagers adopted four at once back in 1999. But that many kids at one time was way out of Wayne's comfort zone.

He stared at the kids in the pool. Sierra and two of her friends, Luci and Ezra, took turns jumping off the diving board. Wayne took a deep breath. "I'll agree to three, but I don't think I could handle four."

I transferred the burgers to a tray and accepted his compromise.

Summer inched by while I completed and resubmitted the paperwork. This time, our application to Homeland Security included the request to adopt three children. In July we broke ground for an addition to our house. We increased the number of bedrooms from three to five. Since our updated home study included this new information, Homeland Security approved us to adopt three children.

Autumn arrived. We continued to wait for Ukraine to reopen adoptions. I clung to God through the wait. Praying, reading the Bible, and journaling my heart out helped me through the discouragement. I also passed countless hours in the FRUA chatroom. I didn't feel like chatting, but I did pay close attention to the chatter.

One morning, in late October the chatroom buzzed with news. I sat at attention and reread the posts making sure I got the story straight. Waiting families like ours were posting their registration numbers and travel dates. I stared at the computer screen shaking my head. Could it be? Did Ukraine reopen the adoption program? My heart raced and my fingers fumbled over the keyboard. Some reported only a limited number of adoptions would be permitted before the end of the year.

Refusing to accept rumors, I tracked the posts about registration numbers and dates. Grabbing the file from my desk, I rifled through documents to find our registration number. I scrolled through the posts, almost knocking my cold coffee over. Steadying the cup with my left hand and maneuvering the mouse with the right, I zeroed in on the most recent posts. Our number landed in the middle of the other numbers posted with travel dates. That could only mean one thing—we were assigned a date too.

I screamed and startled the sleepy kids slurping cereal at the breakfast table behind me. Bypassing our agency, I emailed our facilitator in Ukraine. The clock on my stove read 8:07 a.m. I calculated the time to be about 3:07 p.m. in Kyiv—a good time to reach Andrew. He sent a response within minutes. Relieved someone in Ukraine did something fast, I pounced on his email.

Andrew seemed surprised I knew about an appointment before he did. He sent one of his facilitators to the SDA, so she could check the bulletin board in the lobby. The office posted registration numbers and corresponding travel dates publicly. Andrew promised to contact me as soon as he learned anything.

The next six hours felt longer than the last ten months. I tried to focus on homeschooling, chores, and errands while fighting off the temptation to check my email every five minutes. Around 3:00 p.m. Andrew's email arrived. I held my breath, clicked, and read: "Flach family, come on over. Your appointment date is November 29, 2006."

At long last the wait ended, but the adventure was only beginning.

CHAPTER 21

Children from Hard Places

"I lift up my eyes to the mountains—
where does my help come from? My help comes from the
LORD, the Maker of heaven and earth."

PSALM 121:1-2 NIV

One winter night in 2011, I attempted to settle Slava's busy body down to sleep. Since our return home from Ukraine two months earlier, a bath, pajamas, reading, and bedtime prayers had become our routine. Then I'd shut out the light and lay beside our little boy until he fell asleep. The entire process could take two hours. When his body stilled and his breathing deepened, I'd creep out of his room and collapse into my own bed. My one solace—Slava slept through the night.

On this particular evening, however, he wouldn't settle down. Slava rocked his body back and forth, his head side to side, and tapped a toy hammer on his hand in rhythmic motion. These behaviors, common in children adopted from orphanages, prevented him from being still long enough to fall asleep.

When Slava's eyes finally closed, a sudden loud noise caused him to bolt upright. My dear husband had started a snowmobile in the yard not far from Slava's window. The sound reverberated throughout his bedroom.

Tears spilled down my cheeks. Bleary-eyed from exhaustion, I laid there feeling defeated and begged God to help me. A little hand reached through the darkness and patted my shoulder. Slava. Tears flowed again, this time from a grateful heart. God allowed me to glimpse a tender side of Slava—a part of our rambunctious boy that I hadn't known existed.

Slava never sat still, had no attention span, and zero impulse control. He smashed and banged his way through each day. I wasn't sure we'd survive those first six months. Though we never regretted adopting our son, he did fill our days with trials.

One morning I dumped a crate of wooden blocks on the schoolroom floor. My plan was to occupy Slava long enough to get a Bible lesson done with the bigger kids. He seemed unimpressed until he spotted Daddy's hammer sitting by the door. I watched him pretend to hammer the wooden blocks. The game seemed harmless and kept him busy, so I let him play.

After about twenty minutes, the other kids headed to their bedrooms for reading time. The doctor's office called to confirm an appointment, so I ran into the kitchen to check the calendar. The hammering in the schoolroom continued and I took it as a good sign—Slava hadn't escaped the house. When I returned, he was still hammering. But not on blocks. Slava had switched to the claw end of the hammer. He sat mesmerized as big chunks of wood ripped from the floor.

I gasped. "No, Slava!" I grabbed the hammer from him just as Andrii walked in. He looked at the floor and shook his head. "Dad is not gonna be happy."

"I know. Can you fix it?" Collapsing onto a chair, I buried my face in my hands.

Now fourteen, Andrii had turned into quite a handyman. He ran out to the garage and came back with a sander. After a couple hours, he managed to smooth out the worst parts.

Later that day Wayne assessed the damage. He shook his head, sighed, and headed to the kitchen for dinner. Disasters like the wooden floor debacle were becoming an everyday occurrence. Slava was out of control, and we struggled to parent him. I prayed God would show us how to help our son.

By late May, seven months into survival mode, I stumbled upon *The Connected Child* written by Drs. Karyn Purvis and David Cross. The book became our lifesaver. Right away I implemented some of their strategies—re-dos and time-ins were new approaches for us. But they worked when consistently applied.

As recommended by Purvis and Cross, I took a holistic approach by meeting Slava's needs through nutrition, hydration, physical activity, and connection. In just a few weeks the new techniques started making a difference. Hope sprouted in my heart—hope our family could not only survive but thrive.

Wayne and I both needed to utilize the new "connecting while correcting" parenting tools. Because he seemed too busy to read the book, I ordered Dr. Purvis's DVDs. In the videos, she outlined a path of healing through a trust-based, relationship focused, holistic approach.

One night, after the kids were in bed, Wayne and I curled up on the couch to watch the DVD series. By the end of the first video, my husband looked at me. "Why didn't we know this stuff before?"

"I don't know, but we know it now."

After that, we were on a mission to learn everything we could about parenting kids from hard places—a term Dr. Purvis coined when referring to foster and adoptive children with trauma histories.

Wayne and I practiced Dr. Purvis's method of Trust Based Relational Intervention or TBRI. We also sought professional help for Slava. Sherrie Evans, a local licensed clinical social worker specializing in attachment, became a great support. She was familiar with the work of Dr. Purvis.

Evans explained Sensory Processing Disorder and recommended *The Out-of-Sync Child* by Carol Kranowitz, M.A. I had never heard of SPD before. The book shed some much-needed light onto some of Slava's behaviors.

Since Slava spent the first five years of his life institutionalized, his senses lacked typical stimulation. The senses of smell, sight, sound, taste, and touch send messages to the brain in order to process information about the world around us. Slava's smash and crash personality was driven by his little body craving sensory input. From TBRI and Kranowitz's book, we learned to create a sensory rich environment for our boy.

The social worker also agreed with our suspicion about Slava having a Fetal Alcohol Spectrum Disorder (FASD). She referred us to a developmental pediatrician for formal diagnosis. Per her advice, we also got him evaluated by our school district. Although we home-schooled, the district needed to know Slava's diagnosis. In New York, parents are required to submit quarterly progress reports for each homeschooled child. Because Slava's academic and developmental delays were severe, we wanted it documented in his records.

The above resources became crucial components of our parenting journey. Slava's behaviors were challenging and frustrating. Trauma impacts brain development, which directs behavior. Slava wasn't misbehaving on purpose. He lived in a body wired for survival. When we realized these truths our strategy changed. Instead of parents versus child, we became Team Slava—in it to win it.

A few months after watching the videos, I learned about Empowered to Connect (ETC), a conference for foster and adoptive parents led by Dr. Karyn Purvis. That September, Wayne and I flew from New York to Nashville for the two-day event. We agreed the training was worth every second of our time and every penny spent. Wayne and I returned home from the ETC conference better equipped to parent all our kids.

One gem I gleaned in Nashville came when Dr. Purvis explained that children with an FASD actually have brain damage. A light of liberty glowed within me. I realized the harm done to Slava's brain was the problem, not him. He wasn't a bad kid, and we weren't bad parents. Dr. Purvis's nugget of wisdom freed me to be the mom Slava needed.

The following spring, Evans informed me that Dr. Purvis would be the keynote speaker at an adoption conference in Albany. Because I learned so much from Dr. Purvis in Nashville, I jumped at the opportunity to sit under her teaching again.

My biggest takeaway from the Albany conference pertained to our daughter, Missy, when Dr. Purvis said, "If you find yourself saying 'what were you thinking?' or 'why would you do that?' repeatedly to a child—they are a kid from a hard place. They've experienced trauma."

Glued to my folding chair, surrounded by a hundred people, I felt like the only person in the room. I attended the conference to learn how to better parent Slava. But Dr. Purvis quoted verbatim words I'd spewed at Missy over and over. All these years I thought she misbehaved on purpose when, in reality, her past trauma ruled her poor choices. Guilt and sadness mingled together. The same compassion I'd developed for Slava should have been extended to Missy all along.

The parenting tools Wayne and I learned from Dr. Purvis and ETC brought hope and healing to our family. As we found ways to connect with Slava and earn his trust, his behaviors improved. Wayne and I became ETC Parent Trainers so we could help other families struggling to parent their children from hard places.

Through Empowered to Connect, we gained vital parenting knowledge and skills unique to adoption and foster care. Every foster and adoptive parent must understand the impact of trauma on brain development and behavior. For these parents, traditional parenting methods do not work with our kids and, if used, can actually cause damage.

Wayne and I learned this the hard way. When raising Missy, we had no clue about trauma and its impact. While we knew some of her tragic history, we didn't understand how her childhood experiences fueled the behaviors we dealt with over the twelve years she lived at home. Behavior that presented like disobedience, defiance, and rebellion.

Traditional parenting methods such as time-out, early bedtime, and corporal punishment—even *spare the rod, spoil the child*, did not work with Missy. And as we learned, these techniques did more harm than good. They put distance between us and our daughter instead of close connection.

If I could do it all over again, I would parent our daughter using Trust Based Relational Intervention. We experienced much success using re-dos, time-ins, and providing a high-structure, high-nurture environment with Slava.

We don't have the time and space here to expound upon the ETC principles of empowering, connecting, and correcting. But, if you are a foster or adoptive parent or plan to be, please read *The Connected Child*.

Fetal Alcohol Spectrum Disorder training is of vital importance also. I believe every foster and adoptive parent should educate themselves about FASD. This trauma caused while our children were in the womb affects their brains and bodies. More than four hundred comorbid medical diagnoses accompany an FASD diagnosis. What we, as parents, perceive as behaviors are actually symptoms of brain damage because of prenatal alcohol exposure.

Some invaluable resources I recommend are *Trying Differently Rather Than Harder: Fetal Alcohol Spectrum Disorders* by Diane Malbin and *Guided Growth: Educational and Behavioral Interventions for Children and Teens with Fetal Alcohol Spectrum Disorders and Early Trauma* by Ira J. Chasnoff, MD and Ronald J. Powell, PhD. Websites such as FAFASD.org, FASCETS.org, and ProofAlliance.org provide information and training opportunities. Caregivers can also listen to educational and encouraging content on podcasts such as *FASD Success* and *FASD Hope*.

These tools and strategies will bring hope and healing to your family—they did for mine.

CHAPTER 22

Adopted Children of God

"See what great love the Father has lavished on us, that we should become children of God! And that is what we are!"

1 JOHN 3:1 NIV

A long this journey as adoptive mom and orphan advocate, my eyes have been opened to the many parallels between physical and spiritual adoption. I've been a Christian for more than thirty years. But adopting our children gave me a clear understanding of my salvation and God's redeeming love.

Adoption was created by God and modeled for us in the Bible. Scripture reveals adoption as a divine positioning. Moses was adopted by Pharaoh's daughter. Esther was adopted by her cousin Mordecai. Jesus was adopted by Joseph the carpenter. And we were adopted by God the Father.

If you are a believer in Christ, you've been adopted into the family of God—no longer a spiritual orphan but now a son or daughter with a royal position. When we accepted Christ, we received salvation and so much more. God didn't just save us from sin and hell. Salvation is the greatest gift, but our generous God didn't stop there. He became our Father and gave us a new family, an inheritance, a new name, our identity, His image and new life.

Because God loved us, He adopted us into His family. We are now children of God. For believers, the cross of Christ is our adoption process. Jesus' death on the cross not only saved us from sin but also set us into a new family. We have a Heavenly Father who will never leave us or forsake us. And we become members of the Body of Christ—a Church family.

When Wayne and I adopted our kids, we became their parents and they became our children. Through adoption they not only received a father and mother, but brothers, sisters, grandparents, aunts, uncles, and cousins. Our children are now part of a family.

Through our spiritual adoption, we also have gained an inheritance. Romans 8:17 (NIV) says, "Now if we are children, then we are heirs—heirs of God and co-heirs with Christ the Son of God." By the spirit of adoption, we are positioned as adult sons. Now we have access to all the spiritual wealth of our Heavenly Father.

The children who joined our family through adoption also gained an inheritance—entitling them to the same benefits as our biological kids. To us there was no difference. It's the same with God.

I love this quote from Priscilla Shirer's Bible study, *The Armor of God*: "When the apostle Paul opened his letter to the Ephesians, he spent a majority of this first portion accentuating the grand benefits inherent in salvation. But the depths of God's love in choosing us, adopting us, bestowing grace upon us, and redeeming us are only the beginning of what our relationship with Christ offers. We've also received a vast, boundless, lavish inheritance—one that we did not earn and do not deserve. And Paul wanted to make sure we never forget it. Because if we do, we'll likely live a lifestyle well below our actual means. We'll live within the meager restraints of our earthly resources instead of cashing in on the wealth of our Father."

Are we living according to our inheritance or are we still living as orphans?

When we accept Christ as our Savior, we begin using a new name—Christian. This new name indicates our position as sons and daughters of God. The same thing happens with physical adoption. When we adopted our Ukrainian born kids, they became Flachs. They received new birth certificates with their new names printed on them.

Names indicate identity. Wayne and I took great care in choosing new names for our four Ukrainian children. Andrii and Anna were older when adopted. We opted to keep their first names the same but chose purposeful middle names for them. We gave Andrii the middle name Abraham for two reasons. First, because of Abraham in the Bible. Genesis 12:1 (NIV) says: The LORD had said to Abram, "Go from your country, your people and your father's household to the land I will show you." And Genesis 17:5 (NIV): No longer will you be called Abram; your name will be Abraham, for I have made you a father of many nations. Our son, Andrii, left his birth country and his people to come to a new land—the United States.

God's promise to Abraham in Genesis 17:5 about being a father also resonated with me. Although he was only nine when we adopted him, I believed Andrii would become a great father one day.

More than a dozen years have passed since we adopted him. Now I have the honor of watching Andrii in the role of father. He and his wife, Lauren, welcomed their first child in early 2020. Andrii was born to be a dad. As a young boy, he put family first. I've witnessed him organizing games for the neighborhood kids and teaching drum lessons to children. Andrii has a way of making little ones feel seen and loved.

The second reason we chose Abraham for Andrii's middle name—Abraham Lincoln. A month before we traveled to Ukraine, I read an Abraham Lincoln biography to our kids for homeschool history. This particular Abraham came from humble beginnings but was destined for great things. Our Andrii Abraham came from humble beginnings as well. And God has a great destiny for him too.

To our daughter, Anna, we gave the middle name Esther. First, the Bible indicates that Esther had been an orphan before she became queen: "Mordecai had a cousin named Hadassah, whom he had brought up because she had neither father nor mother. This young woman, who was also known as Esther, had a lovely figure and was beautiful" (Esther 2:7, NIV). Esther started off an orphan, but God had a greater purpose for her. She came to her royal position as part of God's plan to rescue the Jews from annihilation (Esther 4:8).

The Bible says Esther was beautiful and her actions demonstrated bravery. At age seven, Anna was already stunningly beautiful and brave. The other inspiration for the name Esther came from Wayne's Aunt Esther Florez—a pastor's wife and great woman of God. We wanted our Ukrainian princess to be the namesake of such a strong godly lady. Today, Anna Esther is a beautiful young woman who is fiercely faithful to her family and friends.

Jordan Charles did have his first name changed. While his Ukrainian birth certificate listed the first name, Sergey, orphanage staff called him, Serosha. Jordan was three when we adopted him. He'd been at the orphanage since birth. We don't even know who named him—his birth mom, a nurse, or someone at the orphanage.

Our oldest son, Wayne Jr., insisted we change the name. He felt Sergey sounded like "sir gay" and would make the child a target of bullying. Plus, our pastor and his wife had a son adopted from Ukraine whose name is Sergey. It's pronounced surge-E. We figured one Sergey in a small church was enough. Wayne Jr. picked the name Jordan because he liked it. We agreed. Now a teenager, Jordan likes the fact a river in the Bible is named after him.

For Jordan's middle name we chose Charles after Wayne's grandfather. The late Reverend Charles Flach had been a pastor, church

builder, and missionary to Africa. We believed being the namesake
of a mighty man of God would be a blessing over our son.

We prayed for and talked about Slava for three years before
bringing him home. Because everyone in the family knew him
as Slava, we kept his first name. Slava is a shortened version of
Vyacheslav, the name on his Ukrainian birth certificate. Like Jordan,
we have no idea who named him. He too was abandoned at birth
and placed in the orphanage. Some people suggested we change the
name since it's unusual. But, Slava means *glory* and we believe God
will use him for His glory.

Wayne and I chose Joseph for Slava's middle name after Joseph
in the Old Testament. Joseph was taken from his homeland to a new
country because God had a Kingdom purpose for him. We believe
God has a plan for our son too. Slava Joseph is a worshipper at heart.
Most days he can be found in his room praising the Lord with worship music blasting. He loves God and is filled with the Holy Spirit.

Names speak of identity. Identity is another way physical adoption reflects our spiritual adoption. My children are known as Flachs
because that's who they are. Their last name indicates who they
belong to. When we first adopted them sometimes people asked,
"Which ones are your real kids?" My favorite response has always
been, "I'm pretty sure they're all real kids." While their curiosity
seemed harmless, in reality it questioned their identity. Satan, our
enemy, does the same thing to us.

The last thing the devil wants us to know is our true identity in
Christ. And the last thing he wants us to do is walk in it. Planting
seeds of doubt about who we really are is a common strategy of the
devil. Why? Because we were each born with a destiny—a Kingdom
purpose. When we walk in our destiny the Kingdom of God
advances and the enemy loses ground. Our identity is in Christ. We

were created by God. He knew us before we were born. We have a Kingdom purpose assigned to us by God. And He wrote it all out in His book.

> *"Your eyes saw my unformed body; All the days ordained for me were written in your book before one of them came to be."*
>
> PSALM 139:16 NIV

The identity of orphan, both physical and spiritual, includes shame, rejection, and hopelessness. Through adoption the orphan receives a new identity. As sons and daughters, we are redeemed, wanted, loved, and have futures full of hope and purpose. We must walk in our new identity as new creations in Christ.

> *"This means that anyone who belongs to Christ has become a new person. The old life is gone; a new life has begun!"*
>
> 2 CORINTHIANS 5:17 NLT

In addition to receiving new birth certificates, our kids received documents from the federal government declaring them citizens of the United States. As Christians, we become new citizens as well. Philippians 3:20 (NKJV) says, "For our citizenship is in heaven, from which we also eagerly wait for the Savior, the Lord Jesus Christ . . ."

Another similarity between physical adoption and spiritual adoption—appearance. The Bible tells us we are transformed into new creations in Christ. We become His image bearers.

> *"And we all, who with unveiled faces contemplate the Lord's glory, are being transformed into his image with ever-increasing glory, which comes from the Lord, who is the Spirit."*
>
> 2 CORINTHIANS 3:18 NIV

Believers are supposed to look like, act like, and talk like our Daddy. A similar transformation also takes place with adopted children. Sometimes kids resemble their adoptive family. But more often, they sound like them. When one of our biological sons was nineteen and one of our adopted sons was fourteen, they sounded alike. I couldn't tell them apart on the phone.

Our kids even pick up the quirky things we say. Wayne often uses the phrase, "You see what I'm saying?" Now Jordan and Slava say the same thing when explaining something to me. It's funny how they pick up some of our mannerisms. Our adopted children learned to walk the walk and talk the talk of a Flach.

Adoption births new life. An adopted child can go from mere existence and survival in an orphanage or in foster care to thriving in a family. Our adopted children received new lives, which included a new country, new language, new family—new everything. Spiritually adopted children of God receive new life too.

Adoption is a purposeful choice. Birth moms agonize over choosing an adoption plan for their babies. Prospective adoptive families prayerfully comb through pictures and biographies of waiting children. The weight of choosing our children from stacks of files at the SDA office in Kyiv felt overwhelming to us. Wayne and I picked our kids out of a pile of files. But God had already chosen them. And He chose us too. Ephesians 1:4 (NIV) speaks of our spiritual adoption: "For he chose us in him before the creation of the world to be holy and blameless in his sight. In love he predestined us for adoption to sonship through Jesus Christ, in accordance with his pleasure and will . . ."

Spiritual warfare is another common element between spiritual and physical adoption. Spiritual warfare refers to the Christian's battle with the spiritual entity we call Satan, the accuser, or the devil.

Ephesians 6:11-12 (NIV) says, "Put on the full armor of God, so that you can take your stand against the devil's schemes. For our struggle is not against flesh and blood, but against rulers, against the authorities, against the powers of this dark world and against the spiritual forces of evil in the heavenly realms."

Since adoption is the Gospel in action, we should expect spiritual warfare. The enemy is poised and ready to pounce on those walking in the adoption arena. The devil hates when a sinner becomes a son, when the lost get found, when the captive is freed, and when an orphan is set into a family. The adoption journey is paved with opposition and obstacles placed in our path by the enemy to drive us off course.

> *"Be alert and of sober mind. Your enemy the devil prowls around like a roaring lion looking for someone to devour."*
>
> 1 PETER 5:8 NIV

When Christians adopt, their children are lifted out of darkness and brought into the Light of a Christian home. Within this family, children are introduced to their Heavenly Father and Jesus their Savior. My adopted kids have all accepted Christ. This is a huge threat to the kingdom of darkness.

Why is adoption expensive and hard and time consuming and filled with obstacles? Because the enemy hates adoption.

Adoption is redemption—the action of saving or being saved from sin, error, or evil. Adoptive parents are not saviors, but the children they adopt are rescued from evil. Physical adoption is a picture of salvation.

Jesus died on the cross to save us from sin. Left in our sinful state, we'd be headed down a highway to hell. Kids aging out of orphanages and the foster care system face lives of drug abuse, violence, prison, prostitution, human trafficking, and suicide. Hell describes the future of an orphan. But adoption changes everything.

Galatians 4:4-7 describes God's plan of redemption through adoption. He sent his Son to redeem us. Through Jesus we receive adoption to sonship. As his children, we call him, "Daddy."

Adoption requires payment of a ransom. The financial cost to adopt a child is expensive. International adoption comes with an especially high price tag. Wayne and I spent approximately $30,000 to adopt Andrii, Anna, and Jordan in 2006. That whopping number includes fees paid to our agency and translators and the cost of processing our dossier twice, plus airfare for a family of nine, meals, transportation and lodging for six weeks in Ukraine. Three years later we spent almost the same amount to adopt Slava.

For our second adoption, Wayne and I spent four weeks in Ukraine. The entire time felt like we were being held for ransom. Everyday documents needed to be processed and some "fee" required to process them. I wondered if we had a bullseye in the shape of a dollar sign painted on our foreheads. While the price wasn't exorbitant, twenty dollars here, fifty dollars there, a bottle of champagne, box of chocolates or a bouquet of flowers, we had to pay to finish the adoption.

I remember agonizing over the fees when a thought came to mind—God paid a ransom for me. He sacrificed the life of His Son to adopt me into His family. Matthew 20:28 (NIV): " . . . just as the Son of Man did not come to be served, but to serve, and to give his life as a ransom for many." Judas, one of the twelve disciples, is another example. He received thirty pieces of silver to betray Jesus (See Matthew 26:14-16). Ransom is often part of the adoption process. It's not fair. It's not nice. It's warfare.

Adoption requires sacrifice. Families sacrifice time, money, sleep, and most of all—self. Adoption is die-to-self living. Adopting our children required us to lay down our old self-serving lives and pick up new lives of love and sacrifice. When we first brought our kids home, my calendar filled with doctor and dentist appointments, surgeries and specialists. I had more kids to homeschool, more groceries to buy, and more food to cook. Weekend getaways, outings with friends, and time to myself were over for a season.

God made the ultimate sacrifice to adopt us. 1 John 4:10 (NIV): "This is love: not that we loved God, but that he loved us and sent his Son as an atoning sacrifice for our sins." As Christians, we are called to love and lay down our lives for others—this is adoption.

The Gospels instruct believers to count the cost of following Jesus. In Luke 14:33, Jesus says, "In the same way, those of you who do not give up everything you have cannot be my disciples." Adoptive and foster parents must count the cost too—the cost of change.

Life was not the same after we brought our adoptive children home. Family dynamics changed, relationships changed, schedules and routines changed, our interests changed, and even our friendships changed. Prospective parents might assume an adoption will have some impact on their lives. But most are not prepared for the isolating effect adoption can have on their church and community relationships.

After adopting Andrii, Anna, and Jordan, my church experience changed. I found myself in the church nursery with a three-year-old—a place I hadn't been in six years. The first few months Slava was home, Wayne and I had to divide and conquer. He took the older kids to church and I stayed home with our rambunctious five-year-old. Slava needed time to bond with us before we unleashed him into the world outside our home.

The sacrifice and cost associated with adoption might appear scary and uncomfortable. But in the process, we gain much more than we lose. While warfare and sacrifice come with the territory, so do blessings and miracles. In Matthew 10:38-39 (NLT) Jesus said, "If you refuse to take up your cross and follow me, you are not worthy of being mine. If you cling to your life, you will lose it; but if you give up your life for me, you will find it."

As a spiritual adoptee and an adoptive parent, I say—the cost is worth it.

There are numerous parallels between physical and spiritual adoption. The miraculous transformation from orphan to son not only occurs when a parent adopts a child. A Christian also experiences this metamorphosis. Our adoption to sonship releases our identity as children of God. But how many of us live like we're still orphans?

CHAPTER 23

The Orphan Spirit

*"For all who are led by the Spirit of God are children of God. So
you have not received a spirit that makes you fearful slaves . . ."*

ROMANS 8:14-15A NLT

The orphan spirit was first brought to earth by Lucifer when he
was tossed out of heaven. Because of his rebellion, Satan lost
his close relationship with God and his heavenly home. He became
the first orphan. From that time on he has hated families, children,
and babies. The devil has been on an orphan-making mission
ever since.

In Genesis 3, we read about the enemy's first attack on God's
children. The devil spied Adam and Eve in the Garden—a home
they shared with their Father, the one who tossed him out of heaven.
The couple enjoyed everything Satan had lost. And he hated them
for it.

Through the serpent, the orphan spirit targeted Eve. When
tempting her to eat the forbidden fruit, the snake said, "For God
knows that when you eat from it your eyes will be opened, and you
will be like God . . ." The serpent deceived Eve into believing she
didn't have something she already possessed. Eve was already like
God. But the devil planted seeds of doubt. He tricked Eve into
believing God couldn't be trusted. She bought the lie. When Adam
and Eve bit into the fruit, Satan snatched away dominion over the

earth. He gained a kingdom while they lost both intimacy with the Father and their garden home. Adam and Eve became orphaned.

The devil has continued his mission today to steal our identity as God's children and destroy our destiny. The Lord created every person with a kingdom purpose. Psalm 139:16 (NLT) says, "You saw me before I was born. Every day of my life was recorded in your book. Every moment laid out before a single day had passed." Christians who know their true identity are a threat to the kingdom of darkness.

For thousands of years, Satan has deceived God's children into believing and behaving like orphans. A spiritual orphan does not know how to receive the love of God. They live in survival mode instead of trusting their Heavenly Father to care for them. They still act like orphans although they have been adopted into God's family. Recognizing the characteristics of the orphan spirit will enable us to identify Satan's lies and combat them with truth.

Orphans and foster children are prone to carry an orphan spirit. However, that spirit infiltrates the Church as well. We all are vulnerable to the enemy's identity-stealing scheme. Seasoned adoptive and foster parents recognize orphan attitudes in their children—belief systems rooted in shame, fear, self-protection, control, insecurity, and rejection. All these characteristics are common in kids with trauma histories. As Christians, we should be acting like the children of God that we are instead of like rejected orphans. Therefore, we need to identify these paralyzing thought patterns in ourselves.

In this chapter I will unpack the orphan mindsets of shame, fear, and self-protection. Control, insecurity, and rejection issues will be addressed in the next chapter.

Physical orphans have experienced loss and often other forms of harm such as abandonment, abuse, and neglect. Childhood trauma leads to the development of poor self-image, low self-esteem, and shame. In her book, *Nurturing Adoptions: Creating Resilience after Neglect and Trauma,* author Deborah D. Gray states, "Almost all maltreated children think of themselves as bad. In spite of many positive things that people may say about them in terms of later accomplishments, trauma and neglect tend to be foundational in developing a poor self-image."

Shame is the result of sin—our sin or someone's sin against us. When a believer sins, we should feel the conviction of the Holy Spirit which guides us to repent. Repentance leads to the forgiveness of sins. 1 John 1:9 (NIV) says, "If we confess our sins, he is faithful and just and will forgive us our sins and purify us from all unrighteousness." Shame, however, is vastly different than conviction of sin, guilt, or regret. Guilt indicates we did something wrong. Shame tells us we are something wrong. When Christians regret their actions, we know we can repent and be right with God again. Shame, on the other hand, makes us feel as if we have no hope.

Adam and Eve experienced shame after they disobeyed God. In Genesis 3:7-10 we learn that after eating the forbidden fruit their eyes were opened and they realized they were naked. Adam and Eve sewed fig leaves together to cover their nakedness—to cover the shame of their disobedience.

Shame is accompanied by feelings of unworthiness, humiliation, and self-reproach—all part of the enemy's plan to rob us of our God-given identity. Spiritual orphans believe these lies whispered by the enemy, "You are not good enough. You will never measure up to God's standards." They try to either run from shame, or like Adam and Eve, attempt to cover it up—maybe even with religion or good deeds.

Whether caused by being a physical or spiritual orphan, shame is removed through the gradual process of justification and sanctification. Justification is God's act of forgiving our sins and counting us as righteous through faith in Jesus Christ. Sanctification is the continual work of the Holy Spirit within us to transform us into the image of Christ. To be free from shame and the other orphan spirit mindsets, we must submit to the life-long process of sanctification.

"Put off your old self, which belongs to your former manner of life and is corrupt through deceitful desires, and to be renewed in the spirit of your minds, and to put on the new self, created after the likeness of God in true righteousness and holiness."

EPHESIANS 4:22-24 ESV

In the last chapter, I will outline the foundational steps that lead to healing the orphan spirit.

I've experienced Satan's use of shame in my life when he's attempted to silence my voice and obstruct my destiny. I was an incredibly shy child. Looking back now, I believe my timidity stemmed from the divorce of my parents and abandonment by my father. When I was five, he moved out of state and only made rare appearances throughout my childhood. As a little girl, that rejection sent me this message: you are unwanted and unloved. This led to feelings of insecurity and unworthiness.

By first grade, insecurity overwhelmed me. I refused to open my mouth during reading circle time. One by one the other children read out loud, but when it came to my turn, I sat mute in my chair. At first the teacher assumed I could not read, so she placed me in the lowest level reading group. There, too, when my turn came and all eyes were on me, I still sat silent.

However, the assignments I turned in revealed I could read. The teacher came up with a strategy to open my mouth—humiliation. It didn't matter how long I sat in silence, she would not move on to the next student until I read out loud. This caused the other kids to groan when circle time dragged on, which added to my embarrassment. While I don't remember what the teacher said that finally forced my mouth open, I do know what happened next.

When I read, because of fear, the words stumbled forth in slow, mechanical syllables. The teacher refused to accept my feeble attempt at oral reading. She goaded me on by mocking my robotic reading style. While the whole humiliating episode did get me to read out loud, it also gave my classmates license to ridicule me beyond reading circle. Whether at lunch, recess, or gym class, kids would look at me, mimic a robot and laugh. The teasing continued throughout my elementary school years and caused me to feel unwanted and unworthy.

The shame I experienced led to a fear of public speaking and paralyzing insecurity. I was afraid of being humiliated again. My mom credited my first-grade teacher for "getting me out of my shell." But the enemy used the shell of shame in an attempt to rob me of God's plan for my life—a plan that included writing, podcasting, and public speaking.

Today, I am free of the orphan spirit. I'm no longer an orphan but a daughter of my Heavenly Father. He will never leave me or forsake me. I no longer live in fear or insecurity because I have a Daddy whom I can trust.

> "For those who are led by the Spirit of God are the children of God. The Spirit you received does not make you slaves, so that you live in fear again; Rather, the Spirit you received brought about your adoption to sonship. And by him we cry, 'Abba, Father.'"

ROMANS 8:14-15 NIV

Fear, another paralyzing emotion, is caused by the belief that someone or something is dangerous and will cause us harm. Satan planted seeds of fear in the Garden of Eden. He duped Adam and Eve into doubting God's trustworthiness. The tactic worked so well he's been using it on God's children ever since.

Physical orphans and foster children typically live in a constant state of fear. Parents or caregivers who were supposed to love and protect them failed to do so—or worse harmed them. Traumas such as abandonment, neglect, and abuse, impact a child's brain development and neurochemistry, resulting in altered belief systems and increased levels of stress and fear.

As mentioned before, the brain's automatic response to fear is fight, flight, or freeze. Fight can present as frustration, explosive or aggressive behavior, or rebellion. Flight isn't just running away but includes distracting or escaping behaviors such as drug or alcohol abuse, internet addiction, successive relationships, and workaholism. Freeze can appear as defiance, such as the child who refuses to open her mouth during reading circle.

In an earlier chapter I shared about our son Slava's fight and flight behaviors the first night we had him in Ukraine. His out-of-control impulses were fueled by his fear of the unknown—us. I witnessed fear-induced freeze behaviors in another one of our adopted children. When our daughter, Missy, first came to live with us she displayed odd meal-time behavior. While the family passed the potatoes and chatted about our day, Missy zoned out. She'd chew in slow-motion, her big brown eyes wide and dilated. I did not understand this behavior then, but now I know she was paralyzed by fear.

A person living in a state of fear is driven by a lack of trust and the need to be in control of the world around them. Slava used to get stressed out riding in a car. At first, I didn't realize this behavior was rooted in fear. He learned early on what speed limit signs meant and that the speedometer indicated how fast we were going. As a busy mom with eight kids, I always ran late. Backseat-driver Slava monitored my speedometer and the speed limit signs alerting me when I was driving too fast—practically every mile of every trip.

If I acted rushed, Slava would get stressed. I learned to act calm whether stuck behind slow drivers or stopped at long red lights. He also needed to know where we were going and how long it would take to get there.

These experiences were not the typical, "Are we there yet?" variety from a bored kid in the backseat. His questions were rooted in fear. Until his adoption at age five, Slava had never ridden in a car. Every time I buckled him into the backseat, he felt powerless. Fear drove his hypervigilance while I drove the car and he drove me crazy.

When I recognized the cause of his behavior, I prepared him for each car ride. I talked him through what we were doing and where we were going. I also tried to leave earlier, or at least on time, so I wouldn't be tempted to speed. Over time Slava began to trust me and my driving. While he's still a backseat driver, he's now more relaxed. By experience he now knows he is safe, and Mom is trustworthy.

In more than three decades of church attendance, I've encountered countless spiritual orphans living in fight, flight, or freeze mode. Some Christians demonstrate fight behaviors because they fear not being in control. These fighters need to be in charge but don't work well with others. I've witnessed a church member circumvent pastoral authority in an attempt to steal a leadership position in children's ministry.

Other believers respond to fear with flight behaviors. These folks church-hop or avoid regular attendance because they don't want to be told what to do—not even by the conviction of the

Holy Spirit. Not everyone who leaves one congregation for another does so because they fear change—some desire change. But over the years I have seen Christians who can't seem to stay put long enough for God's transforming power to take root in their lives.

Then there are the believers who freeze in response to fear. They exhibit stunted spiritual growth because they fear change. I've observed Christians, myself included, who in some areas appear no different today than ten or twenty years ago. Their faith and their lives bear little or no fruit. Sanctification requires surrender, but they fear relinquishing control to their Heavenly Father.

Both physical and spiritual orphans suffer from fear. Only receiving the love of a perfect Father can remove a spirit of fear. Experiencing that love comes through intimate relationship with the Father. To be in an intimate relationship with God means that we are deeply connected to Him—not a check in once-a-week friendship but a daily, personal relationship. Christians who long to grow in their faith experience intimacy with God through prayer, Bible study, and worship. While these are common practices in the Church, those believers who surrender to the transforming power of the Holy Spirit learn to trust their Father and walk in His truth.

"For God has not given us a spirit of fear, but of power and of love and of a sound mind."

2 TIMOTHY 1:7 NKJV

Physical orphans operate in a mode of self-preservation for survival. They learned to take care of themselves because no one else could be trusted. Stealing, food hoarding, and lying are common fear-driven behaviors. These children know what it feels like to be hungry. They've experienced the uncertainty of not knowing if or when their next meal will come. The fear of starvation causes their survival instinct to kick in—an instinct that doesn't loosen its grip easily.

About a month after we adopted Jordan, I made an eye-opening discovery. While putting him down for a nap, I caught a glimpse of something in the roof of his mouth. My heart hurt when I realized my three-year-old son had stored away some of his lunch for safe keeping.

Jordan came to us malnourished. He gobbled up every morsel of food we gave him. And, as I learned, he'd been stashing some in the roof of his mouth—just in case. These behaviors are common in children from orphanages. They learn to eat fast before someone steals their meager portion. And they hide food because they can't trust more will be available later. Though we stuffed food into Jordan every day since we met him, his brain remained in survival mode.

A physical orphan's mission to survive is understandable. For the spiritual orphan, this behavior can present in a self-absorbed lifestyle. Satan plays on a believer's fear of poverty. Tainted by western culture, we're tempted to strive for more, bigger, and better—money, power, status, and stuff. The devil uses this strategy to lure us into lukewarm Christianity where we prefer comfort over the cross.

> *"I have been crucified with Christ; it is no longer I who live, but Christ lives in me; and the life which I now live in the flesh I live by faith in the Son of God, who loved me and gave Himself for me."*

GALATIANS 2:20 NKJV

Resisting authority and correction are also indicators of an orphan spirit mindset. Orphans and foster children have no control over the cause of their orphanhood. As a result, they do not like to be told what to do and prefer to be in control. Beth Moore, in her

Bible Study, *Breaking Free: The Journey, the Stories* says, "A child who has been forced into things she didn't want to do usually grows up never wanting to be told what to do again—by anyone."

CHAPTER 24

More Characteristics of an Orphan Spirit

"Instead, you received God's Spirit when he adopted you as his own children. Now we call him, 'Abba, Father.' For his Spirit joins with our spirit to affirm that we are God's children."

ROMANS 8:15B-16 NLT

In the previous chapter, we discussed the orphan spirit mindsets of shame, fear, and self-protection. In this chapter we will look at three more characteristics—control, insecurity, and rejection.

Orphans battle to gain some sort of control over their out-of-control lives. We experienced this with our youngest son. Previously I described the challenge we faced with Slava's vocabulary. He was reacting to things beyond his control, as I've already mentioned. We had taken him from the only place he'd ever lived and away from the only people he'd ever known. We knew we were taking him to a better life. But he didn't. He had no understanding we would provide him a life filled with family, love, safety, provision, and a great future. Slava didn't even understand the language we spoke. But he figured out one thing—saying a particular word got a major reaction out of us. Behavior that appeared to be rebellious was really a scared little boy's attempt to gain control of his world. Over time, when Slava experienced safety, he stopped swearing. We earned his trust and disarmed his fear.

Orphans and foster children tend to view parental and authority figures through a negative lens. Each of our five adopted children struggled with any type of verbal correction from my husband and me. Every time we corrected them, they thought we were yelling at them—even if we were not raising our voices. If I asked them to clean their room or take out the garbage they would say, "Stop yelling at me." I wasn't yelling, but they perceived it that way. For kids with trauma backgrounds, raised voices indicate trouble.

When our daughter Melissa was about nineteen, she got into a bit of financial trouble in regard to her car insurance. I noticed she'd received quite a bit of mail from the department of motor vehicles. When asked if something was wrong, she insisted everything was fine. One doesn't receive that many notices from the DMV for no reason, so I called our insurance company. They informed me that Missy's policy had been cancelled due to lack of payment. Worse yet, she had been driving for several weeks without car insurance. In New York state, the DMV fines a driver for every day they have plates on a vehicle without insurance. She had racked up a hefty fine and was only days away from having her license suspended.

Wayne and I sat with Missy to address the situation and help her find a solution. Unfortunately, we did not know about Dr. Purvis's TBRI method back then. When we learned Missy had the money for the insurance, I raised my voice. "Why didn't you pay the bill? What were you thinking? Why didn't you come to us?" Missy's only answer: "I was afraid you'd yell at me." At the time I thought, no one ever died from getting yelled at. But our daughter's trauma drove her to fear our correction more than any other consequence.

Money management and car insurance are abstract concepts that kids with trauma histories have a difficult time comprehending. Missy needed nurturing guidance, not a heavy hand or a loudmouth, to help her navigate adulthood. In his gentle, fatherly way, Wayne helped her through the process of paying her fines and securing new insurance. Now, many years and tons of TBRI training later, I understand the tone and cadence matter. Whether giving instructions, correcting a behavior, or calling them to dinner, I need to modulate my voice or my kids will perceive trouble and resist my authority.

Our loving Heavenly Father created us to be in relationship with Him. But orphans, physical or spiritual, resist being fathered. Submitting to authority is counter-intuitive to their survival instincts. If our perspective of father is tainted by an earthly father who was absent or abusive, our view of our Heavenly Father will be skewed. And, if our birth father did not exemplify our Heavenly Father, we will be vulnerable to an orphan spirit mindset.

As I mentioned before, my birth father divorced my mom and moved to another state. He was a truck driver and barely home with my mom, my older brother, and me anyway. When he moved away, he rarely contacted us. I saw him maybe once a year at the most. Phone calls, letters, and child support were scarce. My mom became a waitress to support us.

The loss of relationship with my father left me feeling rejected, unloved, and unvalued. I never felt like daddy's special, precious, little girl. My mom loved me fiercely, but a mother's love is different than a father's love. An emptiness inside me grew throughout my teen years and impacted my beliefs about myself, others, and the world around me. The abandonment also affected my choices. I traveled the risky road of looking for love in all the wrong places. I was a spiritual orphan.

I believe each person is created with an inner desire to be connected to our Heavenly Father—whether we realize it or not. But when our earthly fathers fail us, we become unable to trust, submit to, or receive love from Father God. In our desperate attempts to find love, the devil lures us away with lies about what love really is.

I was in fifth grade when my mom met a kind man named Kenneth. He eventually became my stepfather. I flat out refused any effort he made to parent me. By age ten I believed I no longer needed a father. Ken treated my mom with love and kindness. She felt secure and happy. I didn't. So, I resisted his fathering for all my growing-up years. Not until I married and became a Christian did I respect Ken as my dad or identify myself as his daughter.

Insecurity also plagues both the physical and spiritual orphan. Orphans often compare themselves with others and never measure up in their own eyes. This belief causes them to be easily offended. They perceive everything as a personal slight.

Children with trauma histories struggle with insecurity. They are vulnerable to feelings of inferiority when comparing themselves with peers. Trauma stunts a child's emotional maturity. Though their biological clock keeps ticking, their emotional clock gets stuck. Four out of our five adopted children presented as much younger than their biological age. This poses difficult parenting challenges when, as teenagers, they begin comparing themselves to their siblings—especially those born into the family.

We experienced this when Missy and Wayne Jr. were both older teens. They are less than one year apart in age, but for a time, miles apart in maturity. Wayne Jr. enjoyed a solid, stable upbringing in a loving home. By the time she joined our family at age nine, Missy experienced abandonment, loss, and abuse. Consequently, her emotional age remained nine for many years.

Wayne and I parented according to maturity, not age. When it came to privileges such as dating and driving, we set rules and boundaries based on what we believed they each could handle. This strategy made sense to us, but not to Missy. The injustice fueled her insecurities. And drove a wedge between sister and brother, daughter and parents. Thankfully, time and maturity have helped heal these relationships.

Christians also struggle with insecurity. God's children often compare themselves to others in the body of Christ. We complain about not being chosen for the worship team or getting overlooked for a leadership position. When we don't receive what we believe we deserve, we take offense. In his book *The Bait of Satan,* author John Bevere refers to offense as one of the most deceptive snares Satan uses against believers.

Insecurity can also present as shyness. My mom used to say that I was so shy if anyone looked at me cross-eyed, I'd cry. I'm not sure this was true. But I do know that not feeling valued or loved by my earthly father made me an insecure little girl. I've already shared how insecurity affected my elementary school years. By high school I would skip class if an oral book report was due.

Yet today I host a podcast and speak in public on a regular basis. What caused this radical change in behavior? I'm no longer a spiritual orphan. I know my identity in Christ. I have a Heavenly Father who loves me and created me for a purpose.

At times the enemy still attempts to silence me. Throughout the writing of this book, he tried to get me to believe I had nothing to say that anyone would want to read. His taunts threatened me when I would sit down to write. *Who do you think you are writing a book? Everyone will laugh at you.* But I persevered because I know I'm a daughter of the Living God. And He called me to write this book. I know God is faithful to equip those He has called.

The final characteristic of the orphan spirit is rejection. Rejection is the lens from which the spiritual orphan views life. They resist God's love because they fear being rejected. The devil spews his lies telling the believer: you are unwanted, unworthy, and unloved. But God's Word says His children are wanted, worthy, and loved.

A young woman I'll call Leah, experienced abandonment at a young age. She was adopted into a loving family, but Satan had already set the stage. Leah's wounds ran so deep she lived in a perpetual cycle of craving and rejecting love. She entered relationships longing to be loved. But Leah's fear of rejection drove her to cheat on her partner. To protect herself, she would reject him before he could reject her. Then she'd move to the next relationship, only to repeat the same cycle.

Spiritual orphans usually have experienced rejection by a parental figure. Their abandonment wounds fester causing them to feel unwanted and unworthy. They crave approval from God and others but fall into the trap of believing their worth and acceptance are based on performance. Any kind of criticism is perceived as rejection. These believers try to earn God's love but feel like they never measure up.

> *"And I am convinced that nothing can ever separate us from God's love. Neither death nor life, neither angels nor demons, neither our fears for today nor our worries about tomorrow— not even the powers of hell can separate us from God's love. No power in the sky above or in the earth below—indeed, nothing in all creation will ever be able to separate us from the love of God that is revealed in Christ Jesus our Lord."*

Romans 8:38-39 NLT

The sin of pride is a central issue for the spiritual orphan. Self-centeredness, resisting authority, control, comparison, and offense are all symptoms of pride. Spiritual orphans have a huge Father-sized void to fill but avoid the Father and attempt to meet this need in other ways. They stack up relationships, careers, accomplishments, and possessions. But these endeavors fail to fill their emptiness. leaving them feeling hollow and orphaned.

In the Parable of the Lost Son (See Luke 15:11-32) we see the orphan spirit manifest in both the natural and spiritual realms. The story describes two sons: one who left home and became an orphan and the other who stayed home but acted like an orphan.

The younger son demanded his inheritance and independence from his father. The boy chose orphanhood over sonship. Only after experiencing poverty for the first time, did the young man recognize his need for a father. The son changed his mind, confessed his sin, and returned home. His father embraced him, demonstrated forgiveness, and restored his position as son.

Most messages I've heard preached from this passage of Scripture only focus on the prodigal son. While the older son remained home, he did so with an orphan attitude. He showed no love for his father or forgiveness toward his brother. In anger he refused to celebrate with the family. In Luke 15:29 (NLT) the older son says, "All these years I've slaved for you and never once refused to do a single thing you told me to do. And in all that time you never gave me even one young goat for a feast with my friends." He saw himself as a slave not a son. His orphan mindset led him to compare himself to his brother. The older son complained his father never gave him a goat. But as the oldest, he was entitled to twice as much as other sons. The boy could have taken a goat anytime he wanted to.

At the beginning of the parable, neither son recognized nor received the love of his father. Orphan attitudes of rejection, comparison, offense, and pride are all displayed in the actions of these two sons. The younger son left the family, choosing to be an orphan. When he remembered the goodness of his father, he realized being a son is better than being a slave. He returned to his father and was adopted back into the family. The older son remained home but acted like an orphan. He failed to recognize his identity and attempted to earn his father's love and inheritance—things he already possessed. The parable ends with the father celebrating the return of one son while beckoning for the other son to step into his sonship.

For most of my life as a believer, I've struggled with the orphan spirit mindset. Disabling shame and fear have driven me to self-protective and controlling behaviors. Insecurity and fear of rejection threatened to silence and sideline me from the abundant life God planned for me.

The enemy has not stopped whispering his identity-robbing lies. Some days, he roars louder than others—but now I know the truth. And because I believe the truth, I'm not as susceptible to his deception. In the next chapter I'll share how to be healed of the orphan spirit so we can walk in the spirit of adoption to sonship.

CHAPTER 25

Healing the Orphan Spirit

"Don't copy the behavior and customs of this world, but let God transform you into a new person by changing the way you think . . ."

ROMANS 12:2 NLT

B efore we look into the healing process for the orphan spirit, we must first understand the spirit of adoption to sonship. Referring to Romans 8:14-17, Warren W. Wiersbe in *The Wiersbe Bible Commentary* states: "The Holy Spirit is also 'the spirit of adoption.' The word adoption in the New Testament means 'being placed as an adult son.' We come into God's family by birth. But the instant we are born into the family, God adopts us and gives us the position of an adult son. A baby cannot walk, speak, make decisions, or draw on the family wealth. But the believer can do all these the instant he is born again."

The spirit of adoption is characterized by the unconditional love of a father and a son who fully embraces that love. Father and son spend time in each other's presence enjoying a relationship of intimacy. The father nurtures his son and the son grows and flourishes through their relationship.

Jesus demonstrated sonship throughout his earthly ministry. He prayed and spent time in the presence of His loving Father. Because of their intimate relationship, Jesus knew he could trust his

Father. He always consulted with Him and submitted to His will. Supernatural, familial love flowed between the Heavenly Father and his beloved Son. This intimate father-son relationship exemplifies the spirit of adoption.

Sons are heirs to their father's wealth. Romans 8:17 says, "Now if we are children, then we are heirs—heirs of God and co-heirs with Christ . . ." Referring to this verse, *The Weirsbe Bible Commentary* states, "A baby cannot sign checks, but the child of God by faith can draw on his spiritual wealth because he is an heir of God and a joint-heir with Christ. The Spirit teaches us from the Word, and then we receive God's wealth by faith. What a thrilling thing it is to have 'the Spirit of adoption' at work in our lives!"

All God's children are entitled to Kingdom wealth. But spiritual orphans live in spiritual poverty because they don't access the riches Jesus died to give us.

The Holy Spirit is the Spirit of Adoption. Before his death and resurrection, Jesus promised the disciples the Holy Spirit—an advocate who would never leave them (John 14:16). The Spirit guides the Christian into all truth (John 14:17). In John 14:18, Jesus said, "No, I will not abandon you as orphans—I will come to you."

Through the Holy Spirit, believers are awakened to our true identity in Christ, healed of the lying orphan spirit mindset, and empowered to live in truth as children of God. We must step into our position as sons and daughters by replacing the orphan spirit with the spirit of adoption.

When we adopted Slava, he exhibited destructive behaviors, didn't know how to play, had difficulty accepting or giving love, and didn't understand what a family was or how to live in one. Our little boy couldn't comprehend that the new life we offered him far outshined the darkness of the institution he'd lived in since birth. Slava did not trust us to take care of him. Instead, fear of the unknown triggered his fight, flight, and freeze survival instincts that I wrote about earlier. Even after we adopted him, Slava still behaved like an orphan.

One morning about a year after his adoption, Slava bounced into our kitchen and perched himself at the counter for breakfast.

I poured milk into his glass, almost spilling it when I looked at his face. His tiny cheek bulged as if he'd stuffed a golf ball inside. "Slava, does your mouth hurt?"

"Yes, very badly," he said as if a swollen cheek were normal.

My boy had an infected tooth. He must have suffered in excruciating pain for days, yet I had no clue. Slava never complained or woke up in the night crying. My heart broke—not just because my son was hurting. But because I realized Slava still believed and behaved like an orphan.

In an orphanage, many children discover a hard truth: no one cares about them. When they're sick or in pain, no one does anything about it. Crying is pointless. So, they stop crying.

Slava never complained about the toothache because his orphanage experience taught him that no one would meet his needs. He learned to live with pain. Slava didn't understand that moms and dads are supposed to come when their children cry or are sick or in pain. Trust, especially where one's parents are concerned, was a foreign concept to him.

From that point on, Wayne and I purposefully demonstrated love and care to Slava. At each meal I'd set a plate in front of him and declare how good parents provide food for their kids. We overdramatized fixing boo-boos and administering cuddles and care when he had a cold. Ten years and a ton of nurturing later, we've managed to disarm most of Slava's fear and earn his trust. Despite all this, I can still catch glimpses of orphan thinking in him. As his parents, we are intentional about reminding Slava of his true identity as our son and as a child of God.

Slava experienced deep levels of inner healing, which came through our parent-child relationship. Over time our constant presence, unconditional love, and God's Word prayed and spoken over him caused his transformation. Slava now believes and behaves like our son.

The process is the same for believers with an orphan spirit. We experience healing from the orphan spirit within an intimate relationship with the Father. Through experiencing His unconditional love and by applying God's Word to our lives, we will be transformed too. Like Slava, we can stop believing and behaving like orphans and embrace the sonship that's been available to us since our adoption.

Being healed of the orphan spirit begins with our relationship with God. Walking in sonship requires more than just believing in God—we must know Him intimately. We need to experience God as our Father, our Abba, Daddy.

Relationships require time and attention to grow. Intimacy with the Father isn't gained through once-a-week church services or occasional prayers for help. This relationship is much like a marriage in which consistent interactions from casual conversations to romantic retreats deepen our understanding, trust, and love for our spouse. Spending time in the Father's presence cultivates this kind of intimacy.

Jesus taught that a relationship with the Father is our number one priority. In Mark 12:30 (NKJV), He said, "And you shall love the LORD your God with all your heart, with all your soul, with all your mind, and with all your strength. This is the first commandment." Pursuing God through regular prayer, Bible study, journaling, Scripture meditation, and attending church services are some ways we come to know and love the Lord in a more personal way.

Within our intimate relationship with God, we experience His unconditional love for us. My husband, Wayne, first introduced me to the Father's love. Though I accepted Christ about a month before we got married, I had no idea what it meant to surrender my life to the Lord. Wayne grew up in a Christian home. I had not. We were young and in love and had not made God a priority in our lives. We were off to a slow start in our walk with the Lord.

Two years later, we rejoiced over the news of expecting our first child. For me, what should have been a season of celebration was shrouded in shame. Guilt and shame over my life before Christ were constant tormentors. One night before bed, through sobs, I confessed to Wayne that I wasn't the nice girl he thought he'd married. And, if he wanted me to go away, I would. My husband is a man of integrity. I felt he didn't deserve someone like me.

Wayne assured me that he wanted me to stay. His response lifted a weight off my heart and relief flooded in. He took my hand and we never looked back.

Wayne's unconditional love and forgiveness toward me was an expression of our Heavenly Father. My husband never made me feel shame. He's never held the past over my head or thrown it back in my face. I didn't deserve his love or forgiveness. And he didn't make me feel as if I had to earn it either. Instead, Wayne has poured special blessings over me ever since. He makes me feel loved, precious, wanted, valued, and treasured. I experienced the unconditional love, forgiveness, and blessings of God as my husband modeled the Gospel for me.

If you are not sure you've ever experienced the unconditional love of the Father, ask Him to show you. He will not hold back His love from you. Many former spiritual orphans, myself included, have testified that we've experienced God's love by a demonstration of His love through another person. For me it was my husband, for others it came from an adoptive or foster parent, or someone who intervened at just the right time. God expresses His love for us in tangible ways as the Holy Spirit flows through others and into our lives.

At Billy Graham's funeral in February 2018, his daughter, Ruth, testified how her daddy demonstrated the love of God to her. I watched the televised event and her testimony moved me to tears. Ruth shared how she was divorced when she met a man at church and began dating—fast and furious. Her grown children did not like him, and both her parents cautioned her to slow it down. Ruth confessed she was stubborn, willful, and sinful. She married the man anyway. Five weeks later she fled the relationship. Ruth drove for two days to see her parents, all the while wondering what they would say. When she arrived, her father was standing in the driveway waiting. Billy Graham wrapped his arms around his daughter and said, "Welcome home." No shame, blame, or condemnation—only unconditional love.

Billy Graham cultivated an intimate relationship with God. He knew the love of the Father and poured that love into his daughter. In Paul's letter to the Ephesians, he prays for Christ to be more and more at home in our hearts as we trust him (Eph. 4:17). This verse speaks of our personal relationship with God. A relationship with roots which go down deep into the soil of God's marvelous love. Then Paul prays for us to have the power to understand how wide, how long, how high, and how deep His love really is. In Ephesians 4:19 Paul writes, "May you experience the love of Christ, though it is so great you will never fully understand it. Then you will be filled with the fullness of life and power that comes from God."

Applying God's Word to our daily lives is an essential key to walking in sonship. Biblical application is more than reading the Word—it's the sustained effort of putting it into practice. Intimacy with the Father opens us up to experience God's love. As we grow in our personal relationship with Him, we learn to apply God's Word to our lives. Through His love and His Word, we are transformed and empowered to live as children of God.

Our beliefs play a key role in healing the orphan spirit mindset. We must allow the Holy Spirit to change our thinking. Romans 12:2 (NLT) says, "Don't copy the behavior and customs of this world, but let God transform you into a new person by changing the way you think. Then you will learn to know God's will for you, which is good and pleasing and perfect." Applying God's Word to our lives transforms our beliefs about ourselves.

The Bible abounds with the truth about who God says we are. We disarm the devil by speaking God's Word. When the enemy starts to whisper in my ear, I combat his lies with God's truth by declaring out loud: "I am forgiven, redeemed, chosen, and adopted. I am holy, blameless, and loved. I am God's handiwork—His masterpiece. I am marked with God's seal. I am seated with Christ in Heavenly realms. I have a kingdom purpose assigned to me by God." Proclaiming our identity in Christ acts as a weapon against the enemy.

The devil is always on the prowl looking to devour the children of God. 1 Peter 5:8 (NIV) says, "Be alert and of sober mind. Your enemy the devil prowls around like a roaring lion looking for someone to devour." Knowing who we are in Christ will protect us from the devil's jaws and free us to walk in our God-given kingdom purposes.

The Armor of God – Our Weapons Against the Orphan Spirit

Our faithful Father provides everything we need to reign victorious over the orphan spirit. Clothed in God's armor, we are equipped to walk in our full identity as sons and daughters.

> *"Finally, be strong in the Lord and in his mighty power. Put on the full armor of God, so that you can take your stand against the devil's schemes. For our struggle is not against flesh and blood, but against the rulers, against the authorities, against the powers of this dark world and against the spiritual forces of evil in the heavenly realms. Therefore, put on the full armor of God, so that when the day of evil comes, you may be able to stand your ground, and after you have done everything, to stand. Stand firm then, with the belt of truth buckled around your waist, with the breastplate of righteousness in place, and with your feet fitted with the readiness that comes from the gospel of peace. In addition to all this, take up the shield of faith, with which you can extinguish all the flaming arrows of the evil one. Take the helmet of salvation and the sword of the Spirit, which is the Word of God."*

EPHESIANS 6:10-17 NIV

Putting on God's armor is the simplest, yet most effective battle strategy. A few years ago, I led a women's Bible study group using *The Armor of God* study by Priscilla Shirer. It was one of the most impactful studies I've ever done. The battle strategies I learned from putting on the armor have helped me secure victory over the enemy. I continue to pray through Ephesians 6:10-17 on a regular basis. I've created note cards, one for each piece of armor, with several correlating scriptures.

On my card for the belt of truth, I've written out multiple verses about truth. By the time I'm finished praying these scriptures out loud—the devil is nowhere around. When Christians wear God's armor and wield the Sword, we are guaranteed victory over the enemy.

In *Breaking Free*, Beth Moore states: "Scripture is the strongest bandage God uses to bind hearts broken in childhood. I believe that those who have fallen victim to abuse are less likely to find instantaneous healing. They are more likely to find progressive healing through the study and application of truth. Renewed minds and positive habits are a necessity to lives pressing onward in victory."

Freedom from the orphan spirit and victory in sonship requires a daily, sometimes moment-by-moment, application of God's Word.

"The weapons we fight with are not the weapons of the world. On the contrary, they have divine power to demolish strongholds. We demolish arguments and every pretension that sets itself up against the knowledge of God, and we take captive every thought to make it obedient to Christ."

2 Corinthians 10:4-5 NIV

As Christians, we either take our thoughts captive to Christ or our thoughts will make us captives. By lining up our thoughts with the Word of God, we can distinguish the difference between truth and lies. The Holy Spirit helps us understand and apply God's Word. Knowing, believing, and living truth is a powerful weapon of war. Truth is the key to freedom.

The steps to healing the orphan spirit begin when a Christian chooses to abide in an intimate relationship with God. From within the safety of this parent-child relationship, we experience our Father's unconditional love. Secure in His love, we find the freedom to walk in sonship.

Daily application of God's Word is required to protect our position as His children and our identity in Christ. Through the Spirit of Adoption, we are transformed into sons and daughters of God—then we will truly be orphans no more.

Testimonies of Former Orphans

In my work as host of the *Orphans No More* radio show and podcast, I've had the privilege of interviewing incredible individuals who share their amazing God-stories. Many of my guests were orphaned or in foster care. I've asked some of them to share a few words about what changed the trajectory of their lives and how they were freed from the orphan spirit mindset so they could walk as sons or daughters of God today. Here are their testimonies:

Mandy Litzke

Mandy Litzke is a former foster youth, adult adoptee, Founder and Executive Director of Safe Harbor Orphan Care Ministries, wife, and mother to seventeen children.

There is a freedom that comes when we freely, intentionally decide to get to know God's character, His heart, and then choose to accept it. We were created for a purpose and a plan—created to have life abundantly. We were created to thrive not strive and merely survive. We thrive as we abide in His grip of grace that comes from His steadfast love—that never lets go, that nothing can separate us from.

We must choose to receive the free (unmerited, unearned, unconditional) gift of God's love. We must choose to take notice of every single good gift from the Father, every ounce of healing grace that He has poured over our lives, every single time that he has spared our lives and recognize the depths that He went to rescue, redeem, and restore us.

It is a deliberate, conscious decision to get up every day and choose this truth over the lies of the enemy. We must choose to put the fear and disbelief behind us, choosing to believe the truth and receive it in our spirits because the perfect love that comes from God casts out all fear. Freedom awaits on the other side of our deliberate *yes* to believe and receive His love.

Daniel Kaggwa

Daniel Kaggwa is a former orphan and now Pastor of Sign of the Dove Ministries Uganda.

I received Jesus under the mango tree where I had intended to commit suicide. That day I learned Jesus loved me enough not to be late—He showed up just in time. I came to realize that God formed man for sonship and for His inheritance after I was taken into Richard's (my schoolmate) family. His father called me *son* and we ate dinner together. I slept in a bed and wore shoes. He bought me a backpack with scholastic materials and drove me to school every morning along with all the other children in his family. This made me feel worthy. Being under the roof of this foster family I found out that I was not isolated. I had no more fear, no insecurity and no longer felt that I had to perform to be accepted. I am thankful for my Lord Jesus and this revelation of God as my Father.

Anu Silas

Anupama Silas Dongardive (Anu Silas) is a former Orphan and Founder and Director of Vanitashray in Maharashtra, India.

I grew up in a huge orphanage after being abandoned by my mother at age ten months. I always longed for a family. Being raised by Godly, Christian dedicated missionaries, I constantly heard of Jesus. Because I was so miserable, lonely, and lost among hundreds of orphans like myself, I was desperate to know personally who this Person, Jesus, is as I was always being told that He cares for me and loves me. Out of desperation I gave my life to Jesus at eight years old, hoping I would see Him. I waited and longed for Him every night as I would cry myself to sleep.

After inviting Jesus into my heart, things began to change in my life. I felt His presence so real, that I no longer cried myself to sleep, and I began to develop a sensitive heart towards others around me. That is the time I also heard God speak to me and called me to serve orphans. Since I had never seen my biological father, never knew what it was to have an earthly father, I struggled greatly. It was hard for me to connect with my Heavenly Father, knowing Him in my mind but to bring that truth into my heart was a challenge.

At age eighteen, I joined Youth With A Mission and received the very powerful truth through the "Father Heart of God" teaching. It was the turning point in my life, which led to healing and restoration. The powerful book, *Father Heart of God,* written by Floyd McClung completely altered my perception of God based on the experiences versus what the Bible says about the Father God. It changed my relationship with God and deepened my spiritual growth. The Lord set me free from misconceptions about God allowing me to understand His true heart, the heart of a father for me. His heart welcoming me to enter into greater intimacy with

God. This was a "God moment" for me, when I understood Him as Father to the fatherless (Psalm 68:5).

Truly God's love and acceptance has been at work in me ever since, enabling me to bring that love and acceptance into the lives of shattered, hurting children. The compassion of the Father has enabled me to overcome insecurity and the devastating effects of some of life's most painful experiences. His Truth has set me free so I can live boldly as a daughter of the Most High God.

His Truth prevails against every ungodly cultural practice, lies, and dictates of the society we live in. He has called me and set me free to set the captives free. He has anointed me to bring healing. As it says in Luke 4:18 (NKJV), "The Spirit of the LORD is upon Me, because he has anointed Me to preach the gospel to the poor; He has sent Me to heal the brokenhearted, to proclaim liberty to the captives and recovery of sight to the blind, to set at liberty those who are oppressed." It is a beautiful journey knowing Him. He has never let go of me.

Jacob Sturges

Jacob Sturges is a Korean adult adoptee and orphan advocate. He is an Orphan Sunday Coordinator and blogger at advocatingfortheorphan. blogspot.com.

Going through my adoption papers a couple years ago, I found a word that I never thought described me—abandoned.

When I learned that "being abandoned" was on my adoption papers, I struggled with wondering if I was truly loved or accepted by others, let alone by God. But in the fall of 2017, I was visiting a church that started a new sermon series about forgiveness and freedom. During this series, they talked about how Christians accept the forgiveness of sin and understand that they are part of God's family so easily. But many Christians struggle with living in freedom of their past. It is an orphan spirit that makes us think we cannot live in the freedom we have in Christ.

What is behind this spirit is shame, blame, abandonment, generational curses of "You do not matter; You do not have value; You are not loved!" When I began to understand about the freedom we have in Christ, it changed my entire life! I am truly loved, not only by others, but by a God who made a way to bring me into His family and call me His child.

I no longer am a physical orphan, but I also do not carry the weight of an orphan spirit. I was brought into a family that loves and cares about me. But I also am brought into a bigger family that loves and cares for me—God's family!

Diana Pryhodko

Diana Prykhodko, whose story is depicted in the feature film, Scars of an Orphan, *is a former Ukrainian orphan and adult adoptee.*

The one thing that set me free from the orphan spirit and turned my life around so that I could walk on a clear path as a daughter of the King is and was the power of the written Word of God. I came to a place in my life where I truly believed that I was worth something. There were days when the enemy's overwhelming lies simply flooded my mind with fear. Fear of being rejected by my adoptive family, fear of never being married, fear of living a life that my birth mother lived, fear that I would become her in the eyes of my own daughter. I saw this pattern and realized Satan had a plan for me, but so did God!

The orphan spirit comes from old ways and habits of thinking. I recognized that it was going to be a battle in my own mind, and therefore I had to renew my mind daily with God's truth. I knew if I didn't get rid of this orphan spirit, I would ultimately end up being a victim for the rest of my life!

George Ebenezer

George Ebenezer is a former orphan and Founder and Visionary of the Child Healing Centre and Beyond Barriers in Bangalore, India.

Having not received love, having had many people who I trusted betray me and break my trust; With constant detachments in relationships—it all came to a point that I could never attach myself in any relationship. I was only getting offended and hurt and becoming very, very sensitive.

This is where my Heavenly Father led me deeper into the LOVE of GOD from a totally new paradigm. He is not waiting for me to change or overcome my weakness. He loves me just as I am. It was at this point when I began to receive love—I began to change. I became secure to be vulnerable. I stepped out to love others, even if they might offend or hurt me. I passionately went forward in loving the hurting and abused, not from my own place of holding baggage, but from the place of being released and loved by HIS everlasting, steadfast, sacrificial LOVE. If there is one truth that began the process of healing, it was the LOVE of GOD.

Oh, how much HE loves me and loves me deeply and tenderly . . . no matter what. I have come to understand that love is not in the shape of a heart but is in the shape of the cross.

Alex Sam

Alex Sam grew up in Emmanuel Orphanage in Kota, India. Today he is a social worker and evangelist in Pakur, Jharkand and author of The Wide Roads of Mumbai: Biography of a Runaway Orphan Boy.

Orphanism is not merely a word—it consists of death, sorrow, sadness, loneliness, and negativity. But when we realize we have a Heavenly Father and He is in control of everything, including us, then we experience peace and acceptance as a child of God.

When I realized everything happened in my life because of a perfect plan from God so I could experience orphanism, be healed, and help others with the same condition, I then experienced much peace of mind and soul.

Many become orphaned because of death. Death is certain for everyone. Technically, we all become orphaned at one stage. But when we realize there is eternal life after death and we will live forever with the Father for eternity, we can overcome the negativity of orphanism.

God's Word gives me much relief. Two of my favorite verses are John 14:18 because Jesus says he will not leave us as orphans and Ephesians 2:10 tells me I am God's masterpiece.

Sandra Flach

Sandra Flach is an adoptive mom and co-founder of Justice For Orphans, a nonprofit ministry on a mission to rally the Church to serve children and families in crisis. JFO's goal is to see every child in a safe, loving family by stabilizing biological families and supporting kinship, foster, and adoptive families. JFO seeks to inspire, educate, and equip the body of Christ to walk out James 1:27.

Sandra hosted the weekly *Orphans No More* radio program on the talk-radio station WDCD The New Light 96.7FM Albany for seven years. When the station switched to an all-music format, Flach transitioned the show to the *Orphans No More* podcast. Her weekly episodes continue to inspire, educate, and encourage foster and adoptive parents and many others through guest interviews and inspirational content.

In 2018, Justice For Orphans implemented CarePortal in the Capital Region of upstate New York. This technology platform equips local churches to serve local children and families through partnerships with county child welfare agencies. Today, Flach serves as the Area Director for CarePortal throughout New York state.

Orphans No More: A Journey Back to the Father is Sandra's first book. In it, she shares her family's adoption journey, what she learned about the orphan spirit mindset, and how to walk in sonship through the spirit of adoption.

She is also the writer and voice for the *Justice For Orphans Minute Spots* heard on the Sound of Life Radio Network throughout New York state. Flach also writes blog and social media posts, speaks at events, and has also been interviewed on other radio and podcasts shows.

Sandra lives in upstate New York with her husband of thirty-four years. They are parents of eight children, five through adoption. Good coffee and dark chocolate are her favorite foods. She loves snuggling up and reading to her five grandchildren. During the summer she can be found on her front porch writing her next book.

Connect with Sandra

Websites	SandraFlach.com
	JusticeFororphansny.org
	Orphansnomorepodcast.com
	sandraflachjfo@gmail.com
Facebook	Sandra Flach-Author
	JusticeForOrphans
Instagram	SandraFlach_JFO
	JusticeForOrphans